Walking in Humility

Seeking to live the life God desires

By

Michael A. Vincent

Walking in Humility
by Michael A. Vincent

Printed in the United States of America

ISBN 1-591607-96-5

Xulon Press
www.XulonPress.com

Xulon Press books are available in bookstores everywhere, and on the Web at www.XulonPress.com

Dedication

I dedicate this book to my parents, Jim and Betty Vincent, who have shown me unconditional love, grace, and support throughout my life.

Acknowledgments

I give praise and thanks to my Lord and Savior Jesus Christ who gave His life so I might have eternal life. That He might use me to contribute in any way to others' lives is only a testimony of His love and grace.

I give thanks to God for my wonderful wife and children who continue to be a constant source of love and encouragement to me in all my endeavors.

Randy Bentele continues to be a great encouragement and example for me. His willingness to partner with me in LifeChange Ministries is an inspiration.

My brothers and sisters in Christ at Living Hope Fellowship continue to provide me with the time and resources to try a variety of projects. I couldn't have finished this book without their patience and prayers.

I am indebted to Dan, Ron, Steve, Joe and Dave for their encouraging words concerning my manuscript. I also thank God for the initial help I received on the manuscript from author Debi Stack.

I thank God for so many people who have invested time and energy into my life. I have had the privilege of having relationships with many men and women who seek to walk humbly with God during my days in college, studies at Seminary, and throughout my ministry.

Table of Contents

Foreword xi
Preface xv
1 The Definition of Humility 17
2 The Salvation of Humility 27
3 The Power of Humility 39
4 The Forgiveness of Humility 51
5 The Obedience of Humility 63
6 The Directions for Humility 75
7 The Dependence of Humility 89
8 The Love of Humility 101
9 The Mandate of Humility 111
10 The Service of Humility 127
11 The Esteem of Humility 139
12 The Stewardship of Humility 149
13 The Exaltation of Humility 163
14 The Victory of Humility 173
Prologue 183
Notes 187

Foreword

Being humble is not easy!

I base this conclusion on nearly four decades of being a pretty self-centered individual. I am sure many of us have felt the same way. Sub-consciously wondering if maybe there was an opening in the Trinity? We live in a world that is self-absorbed. It is easy to see why humility is not a popular trait to wear when all our examples in the world of sports and entertainment promote the idea, "life is all about me."

The insight and hands-on advice included in Mike Vincent's *Walking in Humility* provide a guide for individuals who eagerly desire to live as Spirit-filled believers who have determined that life is not about them.

I have observed Mike as both a colleague and a close friend for close to thirty-five years. You can't find a more honest, genuine, sincere fellow struggler to help steer you to a humble lifestyle. Mike's convictions are born from a thoroughly biblical perspective as he has applied the word in his own life.

A unique focus of *Walking in Humility* is the emphasis on first surrendering your life to Christ because he took the lead as He surrendered His life for all mankind. Only through following Christ's example of surrender can we truly be free to love, lead, serve, steward and be what God created us to be. Then we can taste of the victory that we all long for.

If you want help on how to take your discipleship to another level, to live a holy and others centered life, this book's for you. I expect you will return to these pages again and again to seek Mike's advice and deep instruction on a subject that none of us will master this side of heaven. Will we ever truly be humble? Not here and now, but the pursuit of the lifestyle is worth it.

Dan Brenton
Senior Pastor, Fellowship Bible Church
Roswell, Georgia

Preface

Humility and How I Achieved It
by I. M. Humble.

Let me set the record straight. This is not a book about how I have achieved humility. This manuscript represents my battle with pride and my desire to walk humbly with God as we are commanded in Micah 6:8, "He has told you, O man, what is good; And what does the LORD require of you but to do justice, to love kindness, and to walk humbly with your God?"

I struggle with the sins of pride and arrogance. I know that far too often I think of myself as better than others. If my clothing is nicer than someone else's, thoughts of importance can creep into my mind as a spider making his way through the crack of a door. The key of course is to slam the door fully shut and not allow these thoughts to continue. When these musings occur we must go to the cross and remember God loves each the same, no matter the outer garment.

I recall telling a counselor during my seminary days that my greatest fear going into ministry was my struggle with pride. A pastor has the special privilege of shepherding a flock: a flock that learns to trust him, a flock that comes to hear what God will say through him, a flock that comes and asks advice. Without balance in the strength of the Holy Spirit, a pastor can feel much too important and powerful. One can quickly become proud and arrogant in a such a position. I know the feelings. We all know of stories where pride led to destruction in ministry.

Beginning the Journey

My journey in formally considering humility and pride began the summer before my sophomore year of college. I worked on the college staff of a large church in Kansas City, Missouri. I'm not sure I should call it work. During the day I spent most of my time reading and praying, often falling asleep at the library. We were also assigned to gain training from knowledgeable guest speakers and enjoy special activities together. On weeknights, I led a Bible study, helped organize our weekly college meeting, and goofed off with junior and senior high students. Don't worry—I didn't get paid too much, but it was a great summer of growth in my relationship with Christ.

During my reading that summer, I read Andrew Murray's classic, Humility. This book greatly influenced my life. I desired God to be all in my life, but I didn't really know how. Murray seemed to give me the answer. I must walk in humility. Murray states, "That is, that the first and chief mark of the relationship of man with God, the secret of his blessedness, is the humility and nothingness which leaves God free to be all."[1] I learned if my pursuit is for God to be all in my life, I must venture down the path of humility. It has become a life long quest. I agree with Reformed writer Richard Baxter who wrote in his classic, The Reformed Pastor, "Oh, therefore, be jealous of yourselves; and, amidst all your studies, be sure to study humility."[2]

A Lesson in Humility

I learned an application for my studies soon. When asked to teach a seminar at an upcoming college retreat, I immediately focused on the topic from Murray's book. I went over some notes from my reading, looked up more Scriptures, and felt I had put together something of value. Speaking in front of my peers intimidated me, but I pressed on.

As the time for the retreat drew near, the college staff gathered to share what we planned to teach. Jay, a good friend of mine, announced he would speak about cults. Then another fellow revealed he was going to speak on humility. "Oh, no," I thought, "I'm sunk. How could he take my topic?" In that moment, my brain scrambled to pick a different subject. Nothing new came to mind. When my turn arrived to reveal my topic, I shared my predicament. After discussion, we decided to change my topic to pride, the corollary of humility. Looking up a few more verses on pride would solve the problem. My supervisor approved.

The first night of the retreat at a campground, we sang around a bonfire and had a great time. The next afternoon, people chose which seminar to attend. I sat up shop in a rocky area, anxiously awaiting the crowds which would gather for my teaching debut. Only three people showed up. Most everyone sped over to Jay's seminar on the cults. My heart sank. How appropriate that I spoke on pride and humility for my pride was hurt and I felt humiliated. Finally, my supervisor took pity on me and came as the fifth person in our group. I don't remember much about the actual session, but the experience was a good lesson concerning pride and humility. Since that summer I have pondered many more pages concerning humility and pride.

Several years ago I began writing down a few ideas, and developed a couple of messages on the topic. Finally, as a pastor I took the opportunity to preach about humility, thus further developing my thoughts for this book. My prayer is that through my clash with pride and humility, you may grow in your desire to walk humbly with God. May God bless and enrich your life as you seek to submit yourself more fully to Him in the days ahead.

At the end of each chapter I will have a suggested prayer to encourage you as you further humble yourself before God. Pray these prayers from your heart, or use prayers of your own, to express your desire to walk in humble submission to Him.

A Suggested Prayer:

Oh great and mighty God, as I begin this journey of humility, I ask You to teach me what it means to walk in humility with You. Help me not only to understand the theology of humility, but to actively apply the concept of humility through my daily life. I submit now to the work of Your Spirit. Lead on O King eternal. In Jesus' name, Amen.

Chapter 1

The Definition of Humility

On September 2, 1945, at four minutes past nine, on the deck of the U.S.S. Missouri, the Japanese government finally surrendered to the Allied Powers of the United States, Great Britain, China, and the Soviet Union. General Douglas MacArthur, the Supreme Commander, who would oversee the occupation of Japan, signed for the Allied Powers.

The Japanese government had been searching for a compromise peace earlier in the summer, but President Truman and the Allied Forces would have no part in it. Because of the Japanese attacks on Pearl Harbor, and other aggressions, full surrender was the only option. On July 26, the Potsdam Declaration was delivered to the Japanese government demanding the Japanese Empire surrender immediately or face "prompt and utter destruction." Japan ignored the demand. This led to overwhelming devastation. The U.S. dropped atomic bombs on Hiroshima and Nagasaki on August 6 and 9. Over 150,000 lives were lost. Japan and the world now new the mighty force behind the words of the United States. Surrender was the only reasonable option.[3]

Surrendering to God

Why is it so hard for a boy wrestling in the backyard with his brother, or a commander fighting against all odds on a battlefield, to say, "I surrender?" Why? Because it's a humiliating experience. It's saying, "You are better than me, you are greater than me, you are more powerful than me." It's saying, "No matter what I do, you will defeat me. I have no hope of victory." These statements are repulsive and vile to our egos. Our pride is tortured to admit defeat.

There are times of battle and honor when it's appropriate to die rather than submit to an enemy. This is why we honor our fallen soldiers for their courage. We need heroes who are willing to fight for what they believe in. However, we also understand that when there is no chance of victory, surrender is a reasonable option.

There is no honor in standing up against Almighty God. We can't defeat Him. He is the Almighty Creator who overthrows nations in a moment. But He is not our enemy. He is our holy, benevolent Father who loves us. We should not fight Him, but bow to His power, love and grace.

Until we willfully recognize and admit His infinite superiority over us, along with His unfathomable love toward us, we will never be ready to fully submit to His will and way for our lives. We must honestly admit we have no hope of victory on our own in life. To walk humbly with God we must see He alone brings meaning and salvation to our lives. This attitude must apply to every aspect of our lives if we are to walk in true humility with the King of Kings. A person can never walk in humble obedience to God without first submitting to Him. Even as Jesus submitted to the Father in humility, we too must submit ourselves to the will of the Father.

God in the Flesh

It's an amazing and reverent idea that God became a man. We see this wonderful doctrine in Philippians 2:5-11.

> Have this attitude in yourselves which was also in Christ Jesus, who, although He existed in the form of God, did not regard equality with God a thing to be grasped, but emptied Himself, taking the form of a bondservant, and being made in the likeness of men. And being found in appearance as a man, He humbled Himself by becoming obedient to the point of death, even death on a cross. Therefore also God highly exalted Him, and bestowed on Him the name which is above every name, that at the name of Jesus every knee should bow, of those who are in heaven, and on earth, and under the earth, and that every tongue should confess that Jesus Christ is Lord, to the glory of God the Father.

Jesus left His rightful position of Sonship in heaven to fulfill the plan of God and bring us back into a right relationship with the Father. Only through His death on the cross could we know His salvation for the penalty of our sins. Someone had to be judged because sin had come into the world.[4] Because of our sins, we deserved separation from God for all of eternity. But God loved the world so much that He sent His only true Son to pay the cost of our sins.

Let us remember, Jesus had never sinned.[5] He did not deserve to be crucified and receive the curse and judgment of God. But because of His love for us and obedience to the Father, He humbled Himself, giving up His rights, choosing to die in our place.

Paul declares in Philippians 2:6, "He did not regard equality with God as a thing to be grasped."[6] The word "to grasp" connotes the idea of a robber seizing a candlestick and not letting go. Jesus had every right to not let go of His heavenly glory, but in humility, Jesus left His rightful position at the right hand of the Father and became one of us. He didn't have to keep a death grip on His throne in heaven to prove He was the Son of God.

He Emptied Himself

The inspired writer goes on to say in Philippians 2:7, "He emptied himself." But if Jesus was still fully God, of what did He empty Himself?[7] If any of His holiness or character had defaulted, He was no longer God. How could Jesus empty Himself, and still be fully God?

In coming to earth as a man, Jesus covered His full glory. The word "to empty"[8] means to make void. Jesus voided His effulgent glory without voiding His deity. A.W. Tozer writes, "In His incarnation the Son veiled His deity, but He did not void it."[9] In Colossians 2:9 Paul writes that Jesus was "the fullness of deity in bodily form," but He emptied Himself through limiting His glory.

Covering His Glory

When Superman becomes Clark Kent, he is still Superman. In all aspects, he is fully human as any other reporter looking for a story. Yet, as Superman he can still fly and jump tall buildings. We just can't see him in his fullness until we see the big "S" on his chest and his red cape draped over his shoulders.

When Jesus took on human flesh, He did not cease to be God in any way, but He chose to cover His glory. He had to robe His glory for our sakes. If He didn't, we would be vanquished. In Exodus 33 we learn that no one can see the full glory of God and live to tell about it.[10] Even in the Son, Jesus Christ, we are not allowed to see the brilliant glory of God. We would be totally overwhelmed. We would crumble at the sight of His holiness.

In Jesus we find the glory of God cloaked in the flesh of a man. As described in Philippians 2:7, Jesus took the form of a bondservant to protect us from His resplendence. Now He is Immanuel, God with us.[11] He is among us, and shows us how to live and follow God to the ultimate degree. The glory of God, though not the bounteous glory, dwelt in the midst of humanity, showing us the grace and truth of God. The apostle John writes, "And the Word became flesh, and dwelt among us, and we beheld His glory, glory as of the only begotten from the Father, full of grace and truth" (John 1:14).

Humility Defined

The question for us now is this: As a man, how did Jesus act? Did He use His status and power to overthrow Herod and the Roman establishment? Did He seek fame and fortune by bowing down to offers of wealth and power by Satan?[12] Did He only hobnob with the movers and shakers? Did He show His accusers His glory by calling a legion of angels to wipe out those who sought to wrongly place Him on the cross? No, in every element of His existence on earth, Jesus didn't use His position and power to promote His own agenda. Jesus humbly obeyed God in every aspect of His life.

Jesus had a job to do. As much as some of His followers may have wanted Him to defend Himself and use His power, Jesus focused on His mission and doing the will of the Father. He came to seek and to save the lost.[13] He came to pay for the sins of all through His sacrificial death on the cross. The Lamb of God *had* to be slain. Without the shedding of blood there would be no payment for sins.[14]

Because of His love for the Father and us, Jesus denied Himself and went to the cross. He submitted to the Father's will. In Philippians 2:8 we see His humble obedience. Paul states, "He humbled Himself, by becoming obedient to the point of death, even death on a cross." God in the flesh did not move forward with the agenda of the power brokers of His day. Nor did Jesus sit in a corner and refuse to use the gifts and abilities granted to Him as God's Son. No, Jesus gave us the definition of humility through being obedient to the will of God whatever the cost. Therefore, we define humility as *submissive obedience to God.*

Job's Struggle

Job learned the hard way to submit to God. In the midst of wondering why he had suffered after walking in righteous obedience to God, and feeling the pain of his "friends" doubting his heart and life, Job questioned God's justice. While scrapping the sores on his body, Job thought how could God allow such tragedy to take place, when he deserved a blessing?

First, we must remember that no one really deserves God's blessing. We all deserve God's wrath.[15] It's only by His grace that we are blessed. Scripture clearly teaches all have sinned and are therefore worthy of the wage of sin—death.[16] True justice from God would sentence all to the jail of hell, yet God's mercy is given to all who put their faith in God's way of salvation.

Secondly, God allowed Job to go through tragedy because God had a much greater purpose for Job than material and family blessings. Job was a tool to show the power of God in the spiritual realm. Through Job, God defeated the craftiness of the evil enemy in the spiritual arena. Though Job didn't realize it, in his suffering, God entrusted Job with great responsibility. Satan came to God to test one of God's faithful servants, and God's faithful servant came out victorious. God allowed Satan to take away all of Job's creature comforts, yet Job would not curse God. Even as Job's wife encouraged him to "curse God and die!," Job responded, "You speak as one of the foolish women speaks. Shall we indeed accept good from God and not accept adversity?"[17] Job never cursed God. He would not curse his King.

But Job did question God. The tragedies Job experienced in the midst of his desire to live for God, puzzled Job, as it would any of us. In his final statement to his peers in Job 31, Job states he doesn't understand what he has done wrong to deserve such punishment and disdain by God. In Job 31:35, he cries, "Oh that I had one to hear me! Behold, here is my signature; let the Almighty answer me!" In despair and depression, Job laments the harshness of God and demands an explanation.

Have you ever been in this position? You feel as if you have trusted God, but things haven't turned out like you expected. You've been faithful, but it seems God hasn't carried out His end of the bargain? Cry out to God. Release the bitterness and anger you feel in your soul. Don't let this poison permeate your personhood to the point that bitterness creates unbelief and infidelity. God will listen to your questions. He hears your heartache and pain. This is part of healing in our lives. But we must also remember God still is God. Even when we don't understand His purposes and plans, we should trust His sovereign ways. Are we willing to live a life of humble submission to Almighty God, even when we don't understand His plans, or will we only live for Him if He grants us what we desire?

God heard Job's prayer and grants Job his request. God comes to Job in a whirlwind. In chapters 38-42, God reminds Job of His greatness and power. He is the omniscient, omnipresent, omnipotent God who needs answer to no one. He is the Creator of all and needs not be accountable to Job or any of His creatures. Who does Job really think he is to question the purposes and plans of God for Job's life? Will the faultfinder contend with Almighty God? Through revealing Himself to Job, God in essence puts Job in a submission hold. The bomb has been dropped, but will Job surrender?

A Changed Man

As God reveals Himself, Job has a new perspective on his suffering. He cowers from His brash questions and submits himself to God's purposes and plans. No longer will He question God. He now understands he had underestimated the greatness and power of God. Though Job had experienced great hardship, God was at work in and through his life. After experiencing the presence and power of the Almighty, Job says in Job 40: 4-5, "Behold, I am insignificant; what can I reply to Thee? I lay my hand on my mouth. "Once I have spoken, and I will not answer; Even twice, and I will add no more."

In the presence of God, Job is a changed man. He now knows his wisdom pails in comparison to the wisdom of the all-powerful Creator. It's time to keep his mouth shut. Probably a good idea! As God shows Himself to Job, Job is left speechless in the midst of the grandeur and glory of God.

Now Job is ready to respond with humility. As Job experiences the infinite greatness, wisdom, and power of the Almighty his heart bows before his Master. Job surrenders with humility in Job 42:2-6 and says: "I know that Thou canst do all things, And that no purpose of Thine can be thwarted. 'Who is this that hides counsel without knowledge?' "Therefore I have declared that which I did not understand, Things too wonderful for me, which I did not know." 'Hear, now, and I will speak; I will ask Thee, and do Thou instruct me.' "I have heard of Thee by the hearing of the ear; But now my eye sees Thee; Therefore I retract, and I repent in dust and ashes." Job has now moved into a position of true humility. He recognizes the splendor, power, and nature of his Creator, and submits to His will. This is the same attitude Jesus showed as He submitted to the will of the Father in becoming a man and going to the cross.

A Daily Decision

When we flippantly see God *only* as a benevolent Friend who is there to grant our every need or *only* as a loving Father who comforts us in times of sorrow we will not be ready to live for God. God is also our Lord. He demands and deserves our obedience. God has not created us only so He can do our bidding. No, we are called to follow His commands. Sometimes God has to get our attention by allowing or even causing tragedy in our lives. It's at these times we have the opportunity to cry out to Him in humility, or curse at Him in pride. When a child dies, a pink slip comes, or alcohol overwhelms a family member, we can either recoil in His presence or shake our fist in arrogance. Will we choose to surrender to the Almighty, our loving heavenly Father? We must choose whether we will walk in pride, trusting in our own abilities, or walk in humility, submitting ourselves to the will of God.

Hiding in the Jungle

After hiding in the jungles of Guam for 26 years, Shoichi Yokoi came home to Japan. Most of Yokoi's 22,000 comrades were killed when U.S. forces recaptured Guam in 1944. But Yokoi would not surrender. Rather than give up, he stuck to the Imperial Army's code of never surrender. He lived on the land with a diet of nuts, berries, frogs, snails and rats. But finally he gave in. Upon his return to Japan in 1972, his first words were "It is with much embarrassment that I return." Think of all the blessings this man missed because of his unwillingness to surrender. After he began his life anew, he often discussed survival skills on television programs, wrote a book about his experience, and even unsuccessfully ran for public office.[18]

How many of us are hiding in the jungles of pride and sin? Though we know God is much greater than us, and offers us salvation and peace, we fruitlessly hide from His grace and run from His mercy. We need to give in. We need to bow our knees daily and submit our lives to our loving Father. We must surrender and obey Him.

The Position of Humility

The question for us is this: Are we willing to acknowledge God's infinite greatness and surrender ourselves to Him? Are we willing to be crucified with Christ that God may use us for His glory in whatever way He sees fit?

We must place our selves, our hearts, our souls, our minds—all we are—into the hands of our mighty and loving God that He might do with us as He desires. Once we do this the best we know how, we are ready to walk in humility with God.

A Suggested Prayer:

Almighty and Gracious King, I recognize Your sovereignty and lordship over all of creation, and over every part of my life. Father, I desire to follow in the footsteps of Jesus and submit my life to Your will. Please use my life to give You the most glory and honor, whatever the cost. Enable me, by Your Holy Spirit, to be obedient to the point of death, even death on a cross. In Jesus' name, Amen.

Chapter 2

The Salvation of Humility

Contrition. We heard this word often in the late 1990s as many asked President Clinton to be more contrite and remorseful in his admission of wrong with Monica Lewinsky. His actions were bad enough, but then he went on to lie about his deeds. People wanted to hear from the President of the United States, "I'm sorry. I was wrong." They wanted him to be contrite of heart.

I find it fascinating that many Republicans and Democrats called what President Clinton has done, immoral and reprehensible. Upon what grounds did they declare these actions culpable? On what standard were their judgments based?

Many of the same men and women who accused the president of wrong doing also argue the Ten Commandments should be taken out of our public schools and God should not be involved in government. If we have no foundation for laws and a moral code, from where do we find morality and the definition of right and wrong. If we are not accountable to God and His laws, to whom are we accountable? The Constitution was written by men who believed in a Divine Author to whom we are accountable. Therefore, one might argue, we can't use the Constitution as a measuring stick. How do we decide in our society that President Clinton was wrong, but abortion is okay? How do we know that Kenneth Lay of Enron and Bernie Ebbers of WorldCom are devious in their business practices, but certain styles of music have the right to use profanity and defamation in their lyrics? Who makes the rules?

Many have decided we should make our own rules. Often the rules are rewritten as we go. Politicians find out what polling data produces and then make their own decisions. Right and wrong is based upon majority vote.

Others declare there is a separation between what we do privately and what we do publicly. Some suggest I can make whatever rules for my private life I want. As long as I don't hurt anyone else directly, then what I do is my own business. These adherents may disagree with what Bill Clinton did in the Oval Office, but are only offended by his lie to them and our country. They are aghast not because he lied, but because the lies wrongly affected our public persona of the presidency and hurt many in the process.

Some believe since Bill Clinton was a good president and the economy boomed during his regime, we should forget what he did and move forward. Let's be about the business of the country. For them his abilities and results outweighed his negatives. For them competence, not character, is what matters. The ends justify the means.

Who Makes the Rules?

The problem for us in this morass of issues is "Who makes the rules around here?" Our society is inundated with relativity. Truth is like a lost treasure buried in the depths of the sea. It's still out there, but many are looking in the wrong direction, and some have given up hope that the treasure really exists.

John Leo, in his July 22, 2002 editorial in U.S. News & World Report, sights a recent Zogby International poll of college seniors which found that "73% of the students said that when their professors taught about ethical issues, the usual message was that uniform standards of right and wrong don't exist." Leo quotes Stephen Balch of the National Association of Scholars as saying "the results show the dominance of postmodern thought, including the belief that objective standards are a sham perpetrated by the powerful to serve their own interests." It seems there is no right or wrong, and individuals have a multiple choice option of what they think best fits their situation. This system of thinking is called *Situational Ethics.*

Situational Ethics[19] has made its roost in much of our system today. From our government down to elementary schools, your choice is as good as mine. Charles Colson, the "born-again hatchet man" from the Nixon era, has this observation, "Today, however, few educators—or any other leaders who shape public attitudes—have the audacity to challenge the prevailing assumption that there is no morally binding objective source of authority or truth above the individual."[20]

Should aborted fetuses be used for medical research? Should gays be allowed into the military? Without a basis for truth, these questions and many others are only natural. Without a foundation of right and wrong, the situational answers to these questions are a sensitive and politically correct "yes."

But these questions would not have even been asked years ago. Why? Because there was a Judeo-Christian ethic that protected the rights of the innocent unborn. Because there was a foundation of conviction in our country that unnatural acts which spread disease were wrong. Syndicated columnist Cal Thomas believes,

> ...the general downward spiral of standards has continued because people have not actively implemented the teachings of Christ and his Gospel in their lives. Now, a plurality, if not a majority, build their lives on a foundation of self-interest and moral relativism.[21]

We see relativism not only in major concerns, but also in the fabric of our everyday lives. Just park near a stop sign for several minutes and you will gain a glimpse of how people interpret "stop." Usually, it depends on how important their journey is, or whether or not there is a blue and white in the vicinity, or whether a stop sign at this location is really justified in their thinking.

A Relative Salvation

Many people today pick and choose for themselves their way of salvation. Some feel, "Who cares what the Bible says—what really matters is how I feel about my destiny." The idea of salvation has become relative. People appear free to interpret traditional biblical truth for themselves. Rather than believing the Creator of life, they choose to hope in a salvation which they themselves create. Salvation for many is whatever seems right to their own psyche: reincarnation, being a good person, going to church, believing a loving God won't send anyone to hell. People feel they can make these assumptions because they don't believe God through the Bible is really telling the truth.

What about the thought that all *good* people will go to heaven? But in a field of relativity, who is good? For Adolph Hitler, good was the extermination of a culture. In some countries, good is the dominant, forceful rule of corrupt, socialist regimes. In a context of relativity, who decides what is good? Only a perfect, benevolent, holy, Mind can fathom in every situation and context what is ultimately and objectively good. That mind is the mind of God. Only He is perfectly just, perfectly loving, perfectly good.

Reasons to Believe

If God doesn't exist, there is no reason for order. If God is not, chaos is. Without God, this world would become anarchy. We find examples of this philosophy on the streets of D.C. and L.A.. In some neighborhoods, the police struggle to enforce the law and therefore the law is every man for himself. In these locations, one man's good is another's death from a drive-by shooting. One man's wealth results from the addiction of his neighbors to drugs. However, it will only be a short time until the one time prince of the playground becomes a prisoner in his own system through others taking over his turf.

But chaos doesn't rule the day. We do see order and beauty in the world. There is a Creator who made the heavens and the earth. Love is experienced and relationships are cherished. There is a foundation for truth, values, and morality in our hearts. We do seek justice, even though evil sometimes triumphs. These traits—love, generosity, justice—were not created ex nihlo[22] from the backstages of Hollywood or through laboratory experiments in prestigious universities. These are implanted in our hearts by a divine and holy Creator.

God is seen in the design of the universe.[23] He is seen in the need for governments. He is seen in the love of a mother for her child. And yet, in each of these scenarios our society has denied the existence of a sovereign Creator.

Many have come to believe that man and order just happened. Order came from chaos. Man arose from a murky mess. Therefore, man has become the ultimate survivor in dominating the universe rather than the ultimate creation whom God said was very good. This is rubbish. How do we explain the working of the eye? How do we understand the intricacies of the mind? Dr. Francis Schaeffer, perhaps the best-known Christian thinker of our time, illustrates:

> It is not surprising that my lung system is in correlation to the world's atmosphere, for the same reasonable God made both my lung system and the atmosphere and he put me in this world.[24]

Nations need rules created by a Divine Ruler, yet we have seen in communistic governments, and now often in our own nation, that God is not only denied, but also disdained. The right to practice religion is guaranteed in the First Amendment of our Constitution, but some have executed their right to desecrate Christianity through the National Endowment of the Arts and other actions such as keeping the Bible out of classrooms. Rather than our government only being concerned about not setting up one denomination as our national denomination (like the historic Church of England which a person had to attend or be punished), our government often tries to protect its people from God and religion. While nations such as Russia are putting God back into their curriculum, we continue to treat God as an uncle who isn't spoken of in the family because he embarrasses us.

The result is anarchy. The result is a lack of integrity and honesty in many high officials. Leaders justify bouncing bad checks, giving bribes, and skating around the truth. These debaucheries are a picture of the relativity of our land. Law is what the individual makes it, not what is right or wrong according to God.

We see God also in the wonders of birth and life, but

these have lost their dignity and uniqueness for many. Mothers have lost their call to responsibility as they claim the right to murder. The heat of passion overrides the importance of life. Choice, for many, is an afterthought, not a conviction. Teenagers are told they have no choice - their passions are too strong- just use condoms. Discipline, chastity, and modesty are relics along with morality. Purity and commitment have given in to murder and convenience. These are not principles upon which our families, our society, and ultimately our souls, can survive. Now some seek to play God and defame life through euthanasia and certain types of stem cell research. Don't the ends justify the means? But grade-schoolers and teenagers understand what this means to our society. Life isn't worth much so it must be okay if we kill one another over an argument. If we can take the lives of babies and the sick, why not classmates and teachers?

The Path to Destruction

To say as a society that we have the answers to life, that we are right, that we should be given a chance to run the show, is a path to destruction. It was the path for Lucifer, for Nero, for Hitler, and for Judas. Pride comes before destruction (Proverbs 16:18). As a country we must turn to a Source greater than ourselves for the answers of justice and law. As individuals we must also turn to a greater source of Truth. Each of us must admit we are not perfect. We must admit we can't find truth on our own, and that we are sinners in need of the truth. Bible scholar Carl Henry proclaims,

> 'Thus saith the Lord!' is the only barricade that can save our unheeding generation from inevitable calamity. When all is said

> and tried, modern man's alternatives are either a return to the truth of revelation, even to the Bible as the unpolluted reservoir of the will of God, or an ever deeper plunge into meaninglessness and loss of worth.[25]

What is Sin?

In the summer of 1981, my brother Warren went on an evangelistic missions trip to share the gospel with people in Japan. Through teaching English he sought to tell students about the love of God and the payment Jesus made for the penalty of sins. But there was a problem. The Japanese seemed to have no foundation for truth. Sin truly was a foreign word in their society.

Sin is a foreign word for us today. Because we don't like to feel guilt and remorse, we have watered down ideas of right and wrong, each person becoming his own judge. If we are to discover freedom, peace and joy in our lives, we must first admit our sins. To experience reconciliation and forgiveness in our relationship with God, we must confess we have sinned against God.

What is sin? We have stated that humility is *submissive obedience to God.* Sin, therefore is the opposite—*arrogant disobedience to God.* Sin is consciously or unconsciously living out the statement, "I know better than God, and will act and think according to my own ways rather than God's ways." If a person continues on this course of arrogant disobedience to God, that person will never experience the joy and freedom God offers through Jesus Christ. Without an admission of wrong, there is no hope of salvation. Without a confession of wrong doing and wrong thinking, a person only continues to play around with the platitudes of religion rather than experiencing a life-changing relationship with the holy Son of God. To be saved there must be a sense of remorse and need for repentance.

No Need for Confession

According to Christian pollster George Barna, ninety percent of Americans say they believe in God.[26] About eighty-three percent of our citizenship call themselves Christians. Forty percent of adults attend church and read their Bible outside of church each week. He also tells us twenty-four percent of born-again believers think Jesus sinned while He was on earth and after he was crucified and buried Jesus did not return to life physically.[27]

If we stop and think much about these statistics and the status of our culture, we recognize quickly someone's theology is amuck. Many have redefined Christianity to a social group, or obtuse theological philosophy, rather than a life changing relationship with Jesus Christ.

People want to talk about knowing God's love and spirituality, but also want to write their own commandments and ways of salvation. But we can't come to God on our terms. We must come to Him confessing our need for salvation, and that He alone, by His mercy and grace through the death of His Son, can save us. We can't pull ourselves up by our own bootstraps. We can't climb the corporate ladder to heaven. We can cling only to the cross of Jesus Christ.

John Wesley was a missionary, long before he became the father of Methodism. His evangelistic mission from England to America in 1736 failed. Returning to England two years later, Wesley wrote, "I went to America to convert the Indians; but oh, who will convert me? Who, what is it that will deliver me from this evil heart of unbelief?"[28] Wesley recognized he could not deliver himself, even though He believed in God, was a good person, and in full-time Christian ministry.

Later, on May 24, 1738, at an informal prayer meeting

at Aldersgate Street in London, he submitted his life to Christ and became a Christian. Wesley's journal proclaims,

> In the evening I went very unwillingly to a society in Aldersgate Street, where one was reading Luther's preface to the Epistle of Romans. About a quarter before nine, while he was describing the change which God works in the heart through faith in Christ, I felt my heart strangely warmed. I felt I did trust in Christ, Christ alone for salvation; and an assurance was given to me that he had taken away my sins, even mine, and saved me from the law of sin and death.[29]

To know and experience the salvation of God we must come to grips with our own sins. We must willingly, honestly, and humbly come to God, confessing that He alone can save us from the penalty of our sins. We must come to the cross of Christ with no remnant of our own self-righteousness and piety. Ephesians 2:8-9 says, "For by grace you have been saved through faith; ... it is the gift of God; not as a result of works, that no one should boast." Paul says in Titus 3:5, "He saved us not on the basis of deeds which we have done in righteousness, but according to His mercy." When we come to God we must submit to Him, confess our sins, and say to God, "I was wrong. I can't earn peace, joy, and purpose on my own. I want to know Your love, peace, and the joy of eternal life. Please save me from the eternal punishment which my sins deserve. Forgive me, Lord."

God is Right

It's essential in understanding salvation, that we admit someone other than ourselves is right. "God is right and I am wrong"—this statement must be the basis of our relationship with God. We must admit there is truth, and that Jesus Christ, Truth Himself,[30] came to this world to save sinners—those who did wrong. We must admit that objectivity, along with subjectivity, is proper. We must believe there are standards which one must follow and they come from God through the Bible. If we don't believe these standards, there is no sin, and no need for salvation.

God knew our need so He reached out to us through His Son. Even in our arrogance and pride, our rebellion and sin, He continues to wait patiently for men and women, boys and girls, to confess their need for a Savior and come to His throne of mercy and grace. He knew of our sins, yet He did not turn His back on us. Paul declares in Romans 5:8, "But God demonstrates His love toward us, in that while we were yet sinners, Christ died for us."

True humility in our salvation is recognizing our true state. It's agreeing with God we are sinners unworthy of, yet in need of, the Savior. It's from this posture of humble submission that we gain a true understanding of our predicament and a much greater understanding and appreciation for the salvation God offers us in Jesus Christ.

Chosen by God

Have you fully admitted you can't save yourself? We are not saved by grace plus works, but by grace alone. We don't deserve God's merciful salvation, yet He offers His salvation to each of us in Jesus. He didn't choose us because we were more deserving or extra special. No, we are saved because of His work, mercy, and choosing.

As a little boy I loved football. I watched college football all day Saturday. Sunday mornings I watched Notre Dame highlights. The pros came on Sunday afternoon. I dreamed of playing football with the bigger guys in my neighborhood. But because of my young age, they found excuses to keep me out of the game. I might be injured. I'd get in the way. I'd drop the ball.

Finally my day came. The big boys let me play. I did get kicked. I did get in the way. I did drop the ball several times. I wasn't any good, but they chose me to play with them. The point is they chose me—not because I deserved to play, but because of grace. We've done nothing to merit God's love. No amount of good works will provide a ticket to heaven. We will never obtain the perfection God's holiness demands. But out of love, God chooses us. Being chosen by God is like an NFL team choosing a little boy to be on the roster. Only by His initiative can we receive salvation. We could never earn the right to be on His team.

Admit He is right. Confess you've been wrong. Recognize your sin and come to the cross. Humbly receive the salvation of God.

A Suggested Prayer:

Gracious Lord, I admit I've been wrong. I agree You alone are right. Yours is the way of truth. Mine is the way of sin. I thank You for sending Jesus Christ to pay for the penalty of my sins. I don't want to be separated from You for all of eternity. I embrace Jesus as my Savior. There is nothing I have done to deserve Your gift of salvation, but I thank You for it. In Jesus' name, Amen.

Chapter 3

The Power of Humility

Bob wanted to chop wood, so he went to his local hardware store to ask about the most effective tool for the job. The clerk showed Bob the first option—a small hatchet swung with one hand. The clerk said Bob could chop about four pieces of wood an hour with this tool.

"Okay," said Bob, "But have you got anything better?" Next, the clerk brought out a large axe that took both hands to swing. "This will help you chop about ten pieces of wood in an hour, sir."

"That's much better," said Bob. "I like that. Do you have anything else?"

"Oh, yes," said the clerk. "This is what you really want—a chain saw. You can do about forty pieces an hour with this."

"I'll take it!" Bob replied. "I'll be done in no time."

So Bob went home to try out his new toy, but after a couple of hours he returned to the store disheartened. The same clerk rushed to greet him.

"Back so soon, sir? That chain saw must have worked like a charm."

"Well," said a dejected Bob, "I can't figure it out. The first hour I only chopped four pieces of wood, but blamed that on my inexperience. So I tried again. That time I only chopped two pieces of wood. I became so discouraged that I thought I'd better bring the saw back to you to see if something was wrong with it."

Taking the chain saw from Bob's hands, the clerk fired it up by pulling the starting cord. The chain whipped powerfully around the saw, waiting to chew away at any wood that might cross its path.

"Wow!" Bob exclaimed. "That's amazing! I didn't realize there was so much power in that saw. I just used it to chop wood as you showed me with the axe."

Some people are walking through life trying to chop wood with a chain saw. They have the right tools, but they don't know how to turn on the power. As Tim Allen of the hit television series "Home Improvement" would say, "We need more power!"

God doesn't want us to walk through life becoming more frustrated as we try to live successfully according to our own power. Being constantly worn out when we come home from work is not His will. God doesn't want us to be continually frustrated in our attempts to share the gospel. Nor does He want us to be permanently discouraged because of besetting sins in our lives. God wants us to know joy and purpose in life.[31] The only way we can experience His fullness is by turning on His power. Do you want to live the abundant life God wants for you? Then you must daily live under the power and influence of the Holy Spirit.

Christians have the Spirit

Scripture tells us that when we ask Jesus Christ to forgive us of our sins, God comes into our lives in the person of the Holy Spirit. Romans 8:9 states, "However, you are not in the flesh but in the Spirit, if indeed the Spirit of God dwells in you. But if anyone does not have the Spirit of Christ, he does not belong to Him." Here we see that those who don't have the Holy Spirit in their lives are not Christians. They are of the flesh. 1 John 4:13 also tells us this principle, "By this we know that we abide in Him and He in us, because He has given us of His Spirit."

The Holy Spirit comes into our lives the moment we believe in Jesus Christ as our Savior. Once this happens, He will never leave us. Jesus promises in Hebrews 13:5 that He will never leave us nor forsake us. The Holy Spirit is given to us as a pledge. He is a down payment of all God has for us now and in heaven. We are God's children. He will not abandon us, although we sometimes disobey His commands. Paul writes in Ephesians 1:13-14,

> In Him, you also, after listening to the message of truth, the gospel of your salvation—having also believed, you were sealed in Him with the Holy Spirit of promise, who is given as a pledge of our inheritance, with a view to the redemption of God's own possession, to the praise of His glory.

God is not going to renege on His gift of the Holy Spirit to us. A loving parent doesn't abandon her child when she gets in trouble at school or gets sick in the middle of the night. The loving parent is patient, though frustrated, with the follies and foibles of her child. How much more will God not abandon His children. He is there for us to see we make it all the way to heaven. True believers will persevere to the end because the Holy Spirit has been given to us as a down payment of eternal life with Christ.

Although the Holy Spirit comes into our lives when we receive Jesus into our hearts, we often take control of our lives again. We trust in our own strength and power rather than giving the control of our lives to God. When we allow God to control our lives we are empowered (or filled) with the Holy Spirit (Ephesians 5:18). When we trust in ourselves or the things of the world, we put our own desires and limited knowledge above God's love and will. This is not walking in the power of the Holy Spirit. This is being filled with self-righteousness and pride. We are saying we know how to run our lives better than God.

Giving Him the Keys

On our Missions trip to Romania in 1992, we arrived in Bucharest with the need to catch a train to Craiova, our ultimate destination. The five of us on our team tried to wait patiently for the country leader, Michael, to pick us up from the airport. After a couple hours of waiting, Michael finally arrived. Another team going to a different part of Romania had also landed at the airport, so all of us were ready to get on a bus which would take us to the train station. But now we were running behind schedule. If we didn't hustle, we'd miss the train to eastern Romania and have to wait many hours at the station. Realizing our tight schedule, we frantically made sure all the luggage made it to the bus and hopped aboard.

The bus took off like a rocket. Michael must have promised our bus driver a few extra lei to get us to the train depot by our departure time. The driver threw caution to the wind, winding from one side of the road to the other, running stop lights and dodging pedestrians. It was the ride of a lifetime. When we arrived alive at the depot, we hurriedly jumped from the bus, grabbed luggage from the storage department, not necessarily our own, and ran to the train. We made it to the train as it pulled out of the station. Only such an accomplished and daring bus driver could have gotten us to the station on time.

How ridiculous it would have been if I would have said to Michael, and the bus driver, though I don't know exactly where I am going, or how to get there, I want to drive the bus. Certainly we wouldn't have reached our destination on time. In fact, we may still be looking for the station. Yet, how many of us tell Jesus we want to drive our lives? How many of us grab control of our lives from the One who is the way, the truth, and the life? If we are going to walk in the power of the Holy Spirit, we must allow Jesus to drive. We must allow Him to get behind the wheel. Jesus driving doesn't mean there won't be a few potholes or traffic lights, but it does mean we will arrive at the proper destination at the proper time, according to His will. And unlike the Romanian driver, Jesus won't break any laws in the process.

Who's in Control?

Have you given the keys of your life to God? I'm not asking if you've invited Christ into your life—I assume you've done that. Now I'm asking if you've given Him control. He knows what's best for your life. He knows your needs and concerns, your past and future. Let Almighty God take control of your life so He can lead you down the path of an abundant life full of peace and joy. Let Jesus fill you with His Spirit, so He can empower you to be used for His glory. Humble yourself before Him. Admit He can drive your life better than you can. Ask Him to fill you with His Holy Spirit that you might do His will and walk in His power.

It's like a private in the army who gives up his rights. His sergeant now has the authority to tell him what to do. The private must obey. In this way the private will win the battle against the enemy. The sergeant has more experience and training than the private, and the sergeant cares greatly for his soldiers. He will not lead them astray. He has their best interests at heart. Therefore, the private need only to listen to the orders of the sergeant and obey, and they will win the battle. The private never needs to make the tough decisions. He just needs to follow the orders of the sergeant. In a similar way, we just need to follow our Master and Savior, Jesus, and we will know victory in our lives.

But someone might ask, "If I ask Jesus to control my life, will He?" The answer is a resounding "Yes!" He has already commanded us to be filled with the Holy Spirit. The Bible says in Ephesians 5:18, "And do not be drunk with wine, for that is dissipation, but be filled with the Spirit." Of course, this is not a one-time thing, but a continual filling of His power. We are to keep on being filled with the Holy Spirit. Salvation is a one-time event. We make a decision to ask Jesus to be our Savior. Walking in the Spirit is a continual journey. Anytime we realize we are not full of His Spirit, we are to ask Him to again control our lives. Too often, we get tired of following His will and take back the keys. We think because we have seen Him drive our lives so well, we might be able to do it ourselves. That's what the Bible calls sin. We sin when we quit following His direction and instead trust ourselves and the world.

Responding to Conviction

One of the roles of the Holy Spirit is to raise a red flag in our minds when we sin. We sometimes refer to this as "coming under conviction." Peace and inner joy will be lacking in our lives if we are living in disobedience to God. Our consciences will be pricked, and we may feel guilty. After reading God's Word, we may feel we were wrong in what we said to our wives or how we treated our children. The Holy Spirit may also use someone else, such as a pastor or close friend, to point out sin in our lives.

We should remember however that we should not be too introspective concerning sin. Like the young boy who is so afraid of striking out that he always strikes out, our focus should not be on "not sinning." We should learn from our mistakes, but not wallow in the mud. Satan wants us to dwell upon our faults and weaknesses. He wants us to be so bogged down in our past faults, we are no longer useful to God and His Church. That type of thinking leads to defeatism. That type of thinking restricts Christians to lifestyles of gloom and despair. We are set free in the forgiveness of Christ. Through His pain and suffering we are free to follow God.

Confessing our Sins

When the Holy Spirit makes us aware we have sinned in action, word, or thought we should again seek a right relationship with God through the cross of Jesus. We must agree with God we've sinned. This is confession.

Next, we should thank Him Jesus died on the cross to pay for our sins, and ask Him to take control of our lives again. As we submit our lives and hearts to God, He fills us with His Holy Spirit. Because He has commanded us to be filled with His Spirit, we know by faith, when we ask sincerely, He will fill us.[32] As evangelist Billy Graham states in his classic, The Holy Spirit,

> If you have fulfilled the scriptural requirements for being filled with the Holy Spirit—especially the repentance and submission we have now considered—then you and I can privately say to ourselves, 'By faith I know I am filled with the Holy Spirit.'[33]

The moment you ask, God takes control of your life. He remains in control until you again choose to sin (take back control), knowingly or unknowingly. Sin arrives when we retake control of the driver's seat of our lives. This may be dwelling on an unclean thought, saying an immoral phrase, or committing an unrighteous act.

Walking with Christ in the power of the Holy Spirit is a moment by moment process. Each moment, we must choose if we are going to run the show or allow God to be in control. Remember, if God is in control of our lives, we can't sin because God can't sin. He is holy, blameless, and can't be tempted to sin.[34] We are to be holy, as He is holy.[35] We are to consider ourselves as dead to sin, and alive to God.[36] The only way we can sin is to take back control of our lives. As we grow in Christ, we will not follow our own desires as often, and will allow God to be in charge and make the right choices. We will become increasingly aware we are actually choosing for or against walking with God.

Our Choice

I used to watch television without much conviction. I could watch movies or sitcoms and not feel any pressure to curb what I devoured. As I grew in my Christian walk, the Holy Spirit began to reveal something. He showed me that watching certain programs allowed my mind to be persuaded by lustful and materialistic influences which increased my inclination to sin. I also became convicted that much of the time I spent in front of the television could be used in better ways, such as reading, being with my family, or praying.

A choice confronted me. Would I think, "This is really no big deal. God will forgive me for my lust of the flesh and the eyes. Everyone else watches television, and so I shouldn't be legalistic about it," or would I choose not to watch certain programs, or much television at all?

What choice did I make? I wanted to grow in my relationship with God. I knew many Scripture verses concerning purity of body, mind, and heart.[37] Conviction by the Holy Spirit sat heavy on my heart. For these reasons, I decided to limit both my time in front of the T.V. and the kinds of programs I watched.[38] Usually, I watch only sports, news, and older movies. But even with these we must be careful. Cameramen seem to enjoy showing the sidelines at Dallas Cowboy football games. The program you're watching may not be scandalous, but the commercials can be outrageous. It's tragic how quickly ignominious sites can pop-up on the Internet. We must always be ready to turn our eyes and busy our minds with other thoughts when viewing television or other media.

Allow the Holy Spirit to guide and protect you from the lust of the flesh, the lust of the eyes and the boastful pride of life. Fill your mind with His Word, and you will better know how to keep yourself from falling prey to the schemes of the enemy.

No more Sinful Decisions

With the Holy Spirit residing in our lives, God has given each of us the power to say no to sin. But we must choose to change the channel, or to turn off the television. We must choose to cast off hatred and rebel against greed. We must choose to humble ourselves and obediently follow God's direction.

As we walk in the power of the Holy Spirit, we will know the joy and freedom of living the abundant life. Why? Not only will we know the joy of obeying God in our lives, but we will no longer have the frustration of wrestling with decisions concerning sin. The tough decisions are no longer ours. If we struggle with watching the wrong things on television, with God controlling us, we need not struggle. Jesus wouldn't watch it, so we won't either. If He's in control in our daily battles, we won't have the frustrations of trying to decide whether we should watch it in the first place. God, who is in control, has already made that decision for us. But don't take the keys back from Him. Don't grab the channel-changer and take back control of the TV. To walk in the power of the Spirit, we must allow Him to make the choices. When we do, we will know the joy of humble obedience to our Master.

Then we are set free from the frustration of sin. Jesus will always choose to obey. We no longer need to wrestle with our flesh or the temptations from the past when Jesus is in control. Rather than ache over our decisions and temptations, we are free to have joy and peace as we humbly walk with God.

What will you choose? God gives us the freedom to obey Him in the power of the Holy Spirit. We must daily, moment by moment, turn over our lives to God and walk in obedience. Ask God to fill you with His power. Ask Him to empower you to be used for His glory. Don't rely upon your own strength. Keep on being filled with His Spirit. When you are disobedient again-and all of us struggle with sin-confess your sin. Thank God for His forgiveness through Christ and ask Him again to take control. The reality is we will skirmish with sin. But our goal is to walk in complete separation from sin to give glory to God.[39]

Jesus came to give us an abundant life, but the only way we can know the joy of obedience is by giving Him control of our lives. Humble yourself before Him now. Humble yourself each moment of your life. Commit yourself to serving your King and Lord, and you will know the freedom of being His servant.

A Suggested Prayer:

Lord Jesus, I have sinned against You. Please forgive me. Thank You that I am forgiven through your death on the cross which paid for my sins. I ask You now to again fill me with Your Holy Spirit and take control of my life. I want to live for You. Enable me to walk in humble submission to You, even living as Jesus would live. I also ask, O Gracious Lord, that Your Holy Spirit convict me any time I am tempted to go against Your ways. Enable me to quickly turn from my sins and back to You. When I do sin, convict me of my sins that I might repent, and be empowered by Your Spirit. In Jesus name, Amen.

Chapter 4

The Forgiveness of Humility

After a hard day's work in the yard, I want to take a shower as soon as possible. I work up quite a sweat mowing the grass, pulling weeds, and doing other chores that go along with home ownership. Feeling dirty is something I don't like—especially at bedtime. My wife Kathy appreciates my getting cleaned up after yard work, sports, or other sweaty endeavors. A husband's sweaty body sitting on the couch is generally not good for a marriage.

Most of us in the United States are spoiled because we can bathe or shower whenever we want. Some would say we are obsessed with cleanliness. On a missionary trip to Romania, I learned what it was like not to shower for several days. Their water came on only at certain times of the day. Some days it didn't come on at all. The shower facilities were primitive compared to our own, yet I learned to be thankful just to have the water for a sponge bath. One of the first things I did when I returned home was enjoy a long, hot shower.

As much as we in the West are concerned about keeping physically clean, we seem to care little about being spiritually clean. We would never consider going several days without soaking in a tub or relaxing in a steamy shower. Yet we often go for days, if not weeks, before confessing our sins and allowing Jesus Christ to cleanse us. There are at least two possible reasons why we resist spiritual baths.

Am I Really Dirty?

First, we don't realize we are dirty. Like children after playing outside on a hot summer day, we are oblivious to our need to be washed. Few in our society recognize sin. We used to be a relativistic society that thought "if it doesn't hurt anyone else, it's okay." Now some think "I don't care if I hurt others, I have the right to choose." Former taboos are now up to the individual, no matter what the price.

We have legislated some morality through sin taxes on tobacco and alcohol (known contributors to cancer, higher hospital bills, and traffic accidents). Yet we continue open thinking about abortion and homosexuality, which are just as damaging to the underpinning of our society. Homosexuality is spreading disease, raising hospital rates, and weakening the moral code of our nation so a few might claim their rights.[40] Abortion is costing a generation of people who could contribute greatly to our world. These lost lives could also give love to childless couples who want to adopt but can't because of the vast short-fall of children. Euthanasia and doctor-assisted suicide is not the individual choice it seems. This travesty will affect families dramatically as well as increase greed and selfishness in our already embattled populace.

The guilt of our wrong choices and loss of morality are taking their tolls on all facets of our country. As acclaimed author and psychiatrist Karl Menninger so aptly asked, "Whatever became of sin?"[41]

The church struggles with this disease. Why should we expect the public to agree with God concerning their sins?

That is beyond their capabilities. They are only living as those who are in the flesh. Only believers in Jesus Christ, and seekers whom the Spirit is bringing to conviction, will know the persuasion of the Spirit.

Still, many Christians today are turning Romans 12:1-2 on its head by being conformed to this world instead of transformed by the Word of God. We have long been tarnished by the world's standards. We have fallen prey to committing adultery, gluttony, lying, divorce, gossiping, and other evils. Because of this, we are hardened to sin in our lives, and therefore see no reason to take spiritual baths.

In the 1992 presidential elections, around 40 percent of evangelicals and self-proclaimed born-again Christians made an interesting choice. They felt free to put the economy ahead of moral issues such as homosexuality, promiscuity, and abortion. Why? Because few in the church today feel the debaucheries and consequences of sin.[42] To God, our sins reek, yet we are so used to the foul smell we don't notice the stench. We must recognize our disobedience to God, confess it to God, turn from our sins to God in repentance, and ask God to cleanse us with the blood of Jesus. Then we can thank Him Jesus has washed us clean from the penalty of our sins according to His Word.[43]

For many this process of confession is a very humbling experience. We must acknowledge we are far less than perfect. We can't enjoy our relationship with God if we have known, unconfessed sin, in our lives. Also, because we fail to recognize all our sins, it's important to regularly confess generally that we are sinners. As we confess our sins, then we can thank God for His incredible mercy and love through Jesus. This kind of confession and thanksgiving will catapult our lives to obedience.[44]

We don't like the idea we have fallen short of God's standards. Maybe it was a white lie at the office. So what if we told the gang we had twenty sales last month when we really only had seventeen. Big deal. Everybody does it. Does God care anyway? You bet He does. As believers in Jesus Christ, we should reflect the integrity and honesty of Jesus. We must confess our sins to our holy God. Any time we don't acknowledge our sin to God, we walk around dirty. And it doesn't take too long before we become pathetic. We're more like a pig rolling in the mud than Jesus.

I'm too Sinful

The second reason we don't ask God to cleanse us is we're too embarrassed. Maybe we've gone days without taking a spiritual bath. We've been caught up in a project at work and willingly said, "I'm going to do whatever it takes to get the job done." We've sold our souls to arrogance, ignored our children, and yelled at our spouse.

Now we are convicted (shown) by the Holy Spirit we've been in sin. But this time we feel so guilty, we can't believe our kids, our spouse, and especially God, will forgive us. We try to earn favor with God and others by saying we'll be model Christians for the next two weeks. All the while we carry guilt in our stomachs. The longer guilt remains, the deeper it's buried. One day we finally slough it off and pretend our sin doesn't matter. As long as we try to be good the rest of our lives, everything will be okay. In this scenario, we become hardened to sin. Our sins continue to spiral and compound. We move further and further away from our family and the One we once called Lord.

Compounding our Sins

King David knew the spiral of sin.[45] He should have been on the battlefield, like other kings in the spring, but he stayed home. One evening, he woke up and wondered around on his palace deck. Why did he wake up at evening? This points to a problem. His schedule was off. He was out of sorts. He was living an undisciplined life, asking for trouble.

David peered out into the night and saw a beautiful woman bathing. We want to cry, "David, flee!" but history is already written. King David ordered Bathsheba to come to him. Oh, that David might have confessed his lust to God after gazing at Bathsheba, turned from his sin, and ordered Bathsheba returned to her home. He could have been cleansed of his sin right then. Instead he denied his sin and went on to commit adultery with Bathsheba.

Then, because David was too powerful and too proud to confess his sin of adultery, which fathered a child out of wedlock, he committed murder. Uriah, Bathsheba's husband, was killed on the battlefield because David told Uriah's commander, Joab, to withdraw the troops around Uriah in the heat of war. We see in these events how unconfessed sins compound. If God had not intervened through the prophet Nathan, we don't know what might have happened to David and Israel.

Thankfully, God spoke to David through the prophet Nathan and convicted David of his sin. David now had to choose a response. He could tell Nathan to jump in the nearest lake or order strongmen to throw him to the lions, but David chose the better way. He finally acknowledged his sins to God. He cried out in 2 Samuel 12:13, "I have sinned against the LORD."

How does God respond to David through Nathan? Nathan immediately tells David "The LORD also has taken away your sin; you shall not die."

Forgiveness and Consequences

There are, however, consequences for David's grievous sins. His son born from adultery doesn't live. The nation of Israel and the house of David were judged and experienced years of bloodshed because of David's sins.[46] But David was brought back into fellowship with God (reconciled to God) through the forgiveness of God. Though he committed actions heinous to the heart of God, He is called "a man after God's own heart."[47]

David reflected upon his sins in at least two passages of Scripture. We see an example of a penitent heart in Psalm 51. David confesses his sins against God and asks God to forgive him according to His grace and abundant loving-kindness. Please notice the result of God's forgiveness in verses 12 and 13 - a transformed life. David now wants God to use him to touch others. Because God again reigned supreme in his life, people would see God working in David's life and sinners would come to know God.

Letting God Shine through You

Like David, we often fall prey to our sinful appetites. We must therefore recognize our sins and deal with them through the cross of Christ. The Church is not affecting Her world-the lives of our neighbors and associates- because we are not clean. The light of Christ can't shine through us because we have unconfessed sin in our lives. Christian, repent! If you have committed adultery, if you have lied to your children, if you are not reading the Scriptures, repent! Confess your sin and turn to God. There may be consequences, but then you can have fellowship with God, deal with the consequences, and walk in hope and love with integrity.

It's as if we're in a room with two windows—one facing outside and one facing a large meeting room. The one facing outside allows brilliant sunlight to shine into our room. As long as we allow the sunlight into our room, others in the meeting room will see the sunlight through our inner window.

When we sin, it's like throwing mud on the outside window. The amount of light let into our room is diminished.

If we continue to sin without cleaning the window, the mud becomes thick and hard. The sun may shine brightly outside, but if the mud remains on the window, the light is not only diminished in the room, it's non-existent. Oh, the light is still shining, but the mud prevents it from penetrating the room. The sunlight no longer illuminates our room, and our room, therefore, no longer, gives light to the meeting room where others are gathered. The only way they will see light from our room is if our outer window is cleansed.

The same is true of our lives. When we sin, we put a barrier between us and God. If we continue in sin, without asking Jesus to clean our hearts, the Son will be blocked out totally. Christ will no longer be evident in our lives.

What must we do to get our hearts clean and live an abundant, light-filled life? We must call in the Window Cleaner! The blood of Christ makes our window spotless. We don't have to do spiritual windows. Jesus specializes in keeping our window clean, so His light can shine in and through us. We only have to ask Him to cleanse us. And He's on call 24/7. Jesus is not only available when we say grace before a meal, or during our bedtime prayers, but He's willing and able to cleanse us from our sin anytime. Once we ask Christ to cleanse our lives and forgive our sin, His light will shine through us and influence others.

Sin's Effect

David also contemplates his sins in Psalm 32. Here we see the incredible effects of unconfessed sin. When David kept quiet about his sins, his body wasted away. Guilt and worry in his inner man drained David. He knew in his heart he'd been wrong, yet he tried to hide the sin.

I read the story of an associate pastor who had been hiding a series of adulteress relationships over thirteen years in three different churches.[48] He had hidden his sins from congregations, other pastors, and even his family. But he never could hide his sins from God. Who can hide anything from the omniscient Creator? Yet we stuff our sin into the pit of our stomachs, and its guilt and anxiety torment us. Christian counseling authority Dr. Gary Collins tells us that "whenever tension builds in a person and is not released, the body weakens and eventually breaks down."[49] Counselor Earl Wilson tells the story of a client named Jim.

> Jim was suffering from severe abdominal pain when he first came to the counseling center. He had seen his family doctor and an internal medicine specialist. Neither could diagnose his problem. After several hours of guarded self-disclosure, Jim began to go deeper into himself. He told the counselor about a period of his life that he had never shared with anyone before. He spoke of the emotional energy it took to keep the secrets. He related how he had wanted to talk to God about his shame but that he had felt not even God could forgive or understand. "When the pains in my stomach started," Jim said, "I just knew that I was under a curse. I was sure I had stomach cancer and I thought it was God's way of punishing me. I put off dealing with the guilt for two years just hoping it would go away or that I would die."[50]

No doubt David experienced something similar. Sin's guilt sapped his strength and energy.

God's Cleansing

All of us have things in our lives we wish we wouldn't have done, or said, or even thought. These memories haunt us. They eat away at us. Yet we can't change the past. We can't jump in a car and go back to the future. However, we can bring our past, and all of our sins, before God's throne of grace.

God forgave Abraham for saying that Sarah was his sister—twice![51] God forgave Jacob for lying to his father Isaac.[52] God forgave Moses for hitting the rock rather than speaking to it.[53] Jesus forgave the woman caught in adultery.[54] Jesus forgave Peter for denying Him three times.[55] Jesus forgave Saul of Tarsus for persecuting the Church.[56] We read in Psalm 32 that God forgave David for the incredible sins of adultery and murder. David says that when he acknowledged his sins, God lifted his burden and flooded his soul with the tranquillity of forgiveness.

Are you so arrogant to believe God can't or won't forgive your sins? Do you believe that, though Christ suffered to pay for your sins, you still must punish yourself? Are you so proud to believe that the death of Christ can pay for everyone's sins but yours?

The Bible says unconditionally, "If we confess our sins, He is faithful and righteous to forgive us our sins and to cleanse us from all unrighteousness."[57] The Bible says without exception, "He made Him who knew no sin to be sin on our behalf, that we might become the righteousness of God in Him."[58] The Bible says definitively, "For Christ also died for sins once for all, the just for the unjust, in order that He might bring us to God."[59]

God knows you aren't worthy to be forgiven. None of us are. That's where grace comes in. By grace you've been saved. By grace you've been forgiven. Now you must humbly accept His grace. Will you be so arrogant as to turn away God's gift of forgiveness? Will you say you don't need it? Don't want it? Can't have it? God won't forgive you?

God isn't a liar. Accept His offer of forgiveness—whenever you sin.[60] Don't try to hide your sins. Don't think God won't or can't forgive you. Run to the cross. Run to His throne of grace. Allow the blood of Jesus to cover you.

Take a Bath

Our society prides itself on keeping clean physically. How sad, then, that we choose to walk around spiritually filthy when God offers us spiritual cleansing at any moment of the day! How long has it been since you have taken a spiritual bath? Ask God right now to convict your heart and mind of any sin you are carrying around with you. Committing adultery in the past. Cheating on a test. Lying to get better employment. Being lazy. Turn from your sin to God. Allow the Holy Spirit to minister in your heart and life.

As the Holy Spirit reveals these sins to your heart, agree with God you've sinned against Him and against others. The more specific, the better. Then ask God to forgive you. Through Jesus' death on the cross, God will and has forgiven you! Colossians 2:13-14 states,

> And when you were dead in your transgressions and the uncircumcision of your flesh, He made you alive together with Him, having forgiven us all our transgressions, having canceled out the certificate of debt consisting of decrees against us and which was hostile to us; and He has taken it out of the way, having nailed it to the cross.

There is no more debt for us to pay. Our sins were nailed to the cross. Joyfully and humbly accept His forgiveness and cleansing.

A Suggested Prayer:

Gracious Father, I recognize I am a sinner. I am not worthy of Your forgiveness, but I thank You Jesus died on the cross to pay the penalty of all my sins- even when I ____________________ (name a specific sin if prompted to do so by the Spirit). I don't want to run from You, but to You. With gladness and thanksgiving I accept Jesus' payment for my sins. Continue to fill me with your Spirit and enable me to walk in a right relationship with You. In Jesus name, Amen.

Chapter 5

The Obedience of Humility

In 1944, in the battles of the Philippine Sea and Leyte Gulf, American forces pummeled the attacking Japanese navy. As the U.S. advanced upon Iwo Jima and Okinawa, the Japanese faced one alternative: send their pilots to death. The mission required the pilots to take their aircraft so far out into the Pacific their fuel would run out before they could return to base. Therefore, in this desperate moment, the Japanese pilots committed themselves to kamikaze. Many gave their lives as they hurled their "zeroes" into the U.S. vessels. The human bombs numbered 1,900. Of these, 250 aircraft penetrated Allied air defenses. As willing martyrs for their cause, the pilots sunk 25 ships.[61]

We don't agree with their mission, but their fortitude and commitment deserve respect. Of course all who go to war face the possibility of death. All who participate in defending justice and honor are true heroes and deserve purple hearts and ticker tape parades. We reflect upon the many fire, police, and other personnel who risked their lives, running into the World Trade towers to save others. What incredible heroism! They risked, and many gave, their lives to save others. But few act in war, or on rescue missions, knowing the only alternative is to die.

When Jesus came to earth as a man, His only alternative was to die. Death was His mission. According to the eternal plan of His Father, the only way Christ could seek and save the lost was to be crucified. From that mission, we established our definition of humility in chapter one. The foundation for this definition is Philippians 2:8, "And being found in appearance as a man, He humbled Himself by becoming obedient to the point of death, even death on a cross." We simplified this statement and defined humility as *submissive obedience to God.* Jesus chose crucifixion because He humbly obeyed the will of the Father.

He did the Father's Will

Everything Jesus did was according to the will of the Father. Jesus and the Father were one. Therefore He knew the Father's will perfectly, and completely submitted His humanity and destiny to the Father's mission. This fortitude enabled Jesus to say on the cross, "It is finished." Why? Because He carried out the mission His Father sent Him to do.

We see Jesus focusing on the Father's will in John 4. The disciples had gone to get food in the city. Jesus talked about Himself with the woman at the well. When His disciples returned, they were surprised to see Him talking with a Samaritan woman. They encouraged Him to have something to eat. Jesus tells the disciples, "My food is to do the will of Him who sent me and to accomplish His work."[62] We often think, like the disciples, about how we will get our next meal, or at least what it might be. Immediately after eating breakfast, we begin to think about lunch. Yet Jesus constantly thought about how He could do the work and will of His Father.

Possibly the greatest example of His humble obedience to the Father's will occurred as Jesus faced the cross at Gethsemane in Matthew 26. Jesus and the disciples spent Passover together, partaking in the special supper which commemorated God delivering the Israelites' from bondage in Egypt.

Jesus put new meaning in the bread and the cup. The unleavened bread in the past reminded the people they needed to make haste. Their hasty departure from Egypt didn't allow time for the bread to rise. The cup of wine was a cup of blessing. A continual reminder of God's blessing to His covenant people. Now Jesus announced His new covenant with His chosen people. His broken body and shed blood would pay for their sins.

After the meal the disciples, minus Judas, followed Jesus across the Kidron Valley to the Mount of Olives. The twelve often went there to recline with Jesus, but this would be their last night to see Jesus as they had known Him for three years. He asked James, John, and Peter to join Him in a special spot to pray, the Garden of Gethsemane. This night Jesus had much praying to do. He prayed so long into the morning His disciples couldn't stay awake.

The main struggle in the garden was not the frustrated effort of the followers to stay awake, but the tenacity of Jesus to accomplish the will of the Father. Jesus knew He must fully deny all of His human inclinations. He knew He came to die: to deny Himself and accept the burden of the world's iniquity.

Reasons for Agony

Why was this so hard for Jesus? First, Jesus knew He would go through the most excruciating type of death known to man. The Bible describes Him as "marred more than any other man."[63] The crown of thorns in His brow.

Bones and lead entwined in a whip which tore the skin of His back as He was scourged. Nails driven though His hands and feet. The torture of the slow suffocation of crucifixion. Crucifixion is beyond brutality.[64]

Second, along with the physical abuse He would undergo, Jesus would suffer the anguish of humanity's sin. Let us remember that Jesus in no way deserved this death. We were the ones worthy of the cross, for the Bible says in Romans 6:23 "the wages of sin is death." We earned death due to our practice and heritage of sin. Jesus had never known sin. He was perfect. Hebrews 4:15 proclaims that Jesus was "... one who has been tempted in all things as we are, yet without sin." Judas, Pilate, and others in the gospels proclaimed His perfection.[65]

But Jesus had been sent by the Father to take upon Himself the sins of the world at the cross. His mission was to pay for our sins. John the Baptist exclaimed as Jesus approached him at their first meeting, "Behold, the Lamb of God who takes away the sin of the world!"[66] Hebrews 9:26b states, "... He has been manifested to put away sin by the sacrifice of Himself." All sin, past, present, and future, came upon Jesus at the cross. How foreign this would be to the righteous Savior. Yet, Jesus freely accepted the responsibility laid before Him, thus denying His right to live, He suffered hell for all who would believe on Him. Never could we adequately pay our eternal debts for our unholy lives, except by suffering eternal hell. But Jesus put us before His own earthly desires and went to the cross.

But I believe the physical torment of the cross and the dereliction of sin were not what ultimately led Jesus to question in Gethsemane. His third and chief distress was His nearing departure from His eternal relationship with the Father.[67] Not only would their relationship be severed, but the Father would abruptly turn His back upon His Son, as if Jesus were the One who deserved wrath and punishment.

Jesus would be alone without comfort, peace, or joy. He would experience hell. For the first time in eternity, Jesus would be orphaned from the majesty and effulgence of His Father. Jesus knew this condemnation would last only a short time,[68] yet He was deeply grieved. Luke tells us He prayed with such agony and intensity, His sweat became like drops of blood.

Because of all this, Jesus prayed earnestly and intensely in the garden. He denied all of His human feelings, emotions, and yearnings for survival. Because of His mission and His love for the Father, He committed Himself to do His Father's will no matter what the cost.

His full submission to the will of the Father is seen as, according to Matthew 26:39, Jesus prayed, "My Father, if it is possible, let this cup pass from Me," but then He humbly adds, "yet, not as I will, but as Thou wilt." Three times He prays this prayer of surrender. Here we again find our definition of humility, *submissive obedience to God.* Jesus essentially said this:

> Father, You know My earthly desires and the longings of My heart. In My flesh, I don't want My spirit to be separated from You in any way. Yet I know You have given Me this mission of death and resurrection to achieve salvation for all who will believe in Me. I know You know what's best for the world, Our kingdom, and Your will. Therefore, Father, not My will, but Thy will be done.

During this time of anguish in the garden, Jesus finally and fully committed Himself to the cross. In His spirit, He had known this task from the beginning. Now in His humanity, He recognized it was the time to complete His mission.

The Final Pause

My good friend, Jim Williams, tells the story of going bungee jumping in Australia. As you may recall, Bungee jumping is a past fad where participants are hurled from a high place with only a huge rubber band wrapped around their ankles. Before hitting the ground or water, the bungee springs them back up from their fall. They continue to dangle until the bungee stops bouncing and they are rescued by an attendant.

Jim had never done this before, but he desired to give it a try. He believed the time was right on a trip he took to Australia. Since this death defying stunt was created in New Zealand, he thought it would be significant for him to try it while he was "Down Under." He had his mission. When he arrived in Australia, he learned of a wonderful place to jump. At the right opportunity, he wandered off by himself to accomplish his goal.

The bungee jumping location was on a bridge set back into a dense forest. To reach the overhanging bridge, Jim had to walk up thirteen stories of steps with scarce railing. After being weighed, Jim began his trek up the steps. Before long, however, his anxiety reminded him of his fear of heights. As he approached the halfway point on the stairs, something stopped Jim in his tracks. His legs froze. He was going up too high. The steps were too narrow. Already he was about seventy-five feet up in the air. "This is crazy" he thought, and he turned around and began to descend.

However, after going down one flight, he paused. "One of my goals in coming to Australia was to bungee jump. Would I get this close, and let fear snatch away the victory?" In a moment, peace overcame his trembling, and his resolve moved him up the next eighty-five feet. After short instructions and a brief countdown from five, Jim hurled himself through the air at sixty-five miles an hour, only to be saved from death by a huge rubber band. He was rescued minutes later from his dangling predicament by an assistant in a row boat. Jim was safe and had completed his task.[69]

The Garden of Gethsemane for Jesus was His pause on the step. The task ahead was monumental, yet the task ahead had been given by the One He loved. Therefore, with great resolve, He went forward with a peace that surpasses all comprehension. He had made up His mind. He would go to the cross. This is humble obedience.

We observe the resolution of Jesus when He awakened the three disciples after His time of prayer. The Son of God asks, "Are you still sleeping and taking your rest? Behold, the hour is at hand and the Son of Man is being betrayed into the hands of sinners. Arise, let us be going; behold, the one who betrays Me is at hand!"[70] There is no timidity in His voice, only commitment. Jesus was ready to carry out His ultimate act of humble obedience.

More than Words

Humility is not just making a verbal commitment. It's not just saying "Thy will be done." To have humility, we must step out in faith, being fully resolved to carry out our commitment to the Father. After praying and seeking the Father, Jesus was ready to be delivered into the hands of unrighteous men. A kiss betrayed Him. His disciples left Him. The crowd mocked and spat upon Him. A crown of unyielding thorns pierced His brow. The crowds screamed, "Crucify Him!" in substitution for the murderer Barabbas. The whip gouged His back with fragments of bone. He walked up the Via Dolorosa[71] while people unmercifully mocked and yelled obscenities at Him. Nailed to a cross, the Son of God hung at Golgotha between two criminals, counted as a criminal Himself. Even these men hurled abuse at the King of the Jews. Many demanded Jesus save His life since He had already saved the lives of others. "Prove Yourself by coming down from the cross," they shouted.[72]

Could He have done so? Could He have come from the cross and made fools of all His jesters? I don't choose to limit God by saying He couldn't have come down from the cross supernaturally. Yet Jesus was fully and completely committed to His statement in the garden, "Thy will be done." There was no turning back, no walking down the stairs. Humility was about to win the victory planned before the foundation of the earth. Jesus finished His mission through humble obedience.

A Life of Crucifixion

Dietrich Bonhoffer said in his classic work, The Cost of Discipleship, "The Christian life is a life of crucifixion."[73] C.T. Studd, the famous cricketeer in England, gave up a life of wealth and fame to become a missionary to Africa. He proclaimed, "If Jesus Christ be God and died for me then no sacrifice can be too great for me to make for Him."[74]

Jesus told us in Matthew 16:24, "If anyone wishes to come after Me, let him deny himself, take up His cross, and follow Me."[75] The apostle Paul wrote in Galatians 2:20, "I have been crucified with Christ; and it's no longer I who live, but Christ lives in me."

The disciple of Christ must go to his cross of self-denial, fighting his humanness and flesh, and commit himself to obey God no matter what the cost. Our cross is our selfishness, our pride, our humanness. We must turn our lives over to God. We must give up our rights to comfort and leisure. We must deny that we are free to live as we choose. Allan Bloom, late professor at the University of Chicago, postulated, "To say, 'I've got my rights' is as instinctive with Americans as breathing...."[76] This is not the way of the disciple. Jesus stated in Matthew 16:25, "For whoever wishes to save his life shall lose it; but whoever loses his life for My sake shall find it."

What is God calling you to give up for His glory? Maybe you need to set aside your fear and talk with your neighbor about Christ and coming to church? Maybe you need to turn off your TV and spend more time in prayer? Maybe you need to give more money to missions and spend less on dining out?

True fulfillment comes not from seeking wealth and platitudes. Andrew Murray writes, "Only as we approach God in humility, meekness, patience, and entire resignation to His will does He reveal to us the blessings in obedience."[77] The abundance and joy of the resurrection come from being crucified with Christ. When we are crucified to self, we forget ourselves. When we are crucified to self, we are free to love God with all our hearts and to serve others. As author Jerry White states, we must be able to put on our bulletin board, "Resolved: To follow God with all my heart. Resolved also: Whether others do or not, I will."[78] Only as our flesh is crucified, can we know the satisfaction of being fulfilled in doing the Father's will.

Wholly Committed

D.L. Moody was a young man who came from the country. While working as a shoe clerk, he met Christ through his Sunday school teacher. Eventually Moody founded his own Sunday School in Chicago, and its enrollment grew to over 1,000 students. Later, Moody traveled to England. He wanted his life to be influenced by some of the great London preachers like Parker and Spurgeon. Yet, what stuck with him during his trip was what Henry Varley, a worker with Spurgeon, said during a prayer meeting. Varley said, "The world has yet to see what God can do with one man wholly committed to Him."[79]

This phrase constantly called Moody to commit his life to God and walk in humble obedience. As we know today, God mightily used this man to reach the world through his preaching, Bible schools, and church. Millions today are affected through the ministries Moody began as he trusted the Lord.

Why did God use Dwight Moody to change the world? Did God use Moody because he was such a great man? No. God used Moody because Moody recognized not that he was a great man, but that he served a great God. Moody constantly submitted His life to the control of the Holy Spirit. He lived a kamikaze lifestyle. He didn't worry about his own needs and desires, but sought to do the will of God.

What will God do through your life as you consistently humble yourself before Him and submit yourself to the leading and power of the Holy Spirit? Raise godly children? Start a Bible Study at work? Lead a family member to Christ? Pray daily for your Pastor? Develop a youth ministry which will reach out to your community?

Be crucified with Christ. Victory comes for us only as we deny ourselves, take up our cross daily and follow Him. Victory comes for us as we commit ourselves to kamikaze in this life. That was Christ's mission—to come and die. It's our mission as well, for such humble obedience leads not only to the crucifixion of our flesh, but to resurrection power. It's only as we are dead to ourselves and filled with Christ that others will see and experience the resurrection power of Christ which will change lives and the world.

A Suggested Prayer:

Father, give me the humility and courage to commit kamikaze for the sake of the gospel. Enable me to make the hard and sacrificial choices of denying my fleshly desires and living for You. Please do this so Jesus will live, and change the world, through me. In the name of the One who gave His life for me, Amen.

Chapter 6

The Directions for Humility

Several years ago, My wife Kathy and I received an invitation to a pastors and wives' luncheon. We felt excited for a chance to get away together without our two children. My mother graciously traveled sixty miles to watch the kids.

As Kathy and I drove merrily down the highway, she interjected in a joking way, "Dear, do you know where you're going?"

I responded with sarcasm. "No, honey. I don't have any idea where I'm going." But of course I knew exactly where I was going. The directions lay beside me in the car. "How silly for someone to drive and not know where he's going," I thought.

Kathy's suspicion of our going the wrong way continued. After a few moments, she picked up the written directions laying on the seat. She read them and sighed.

"Mike, I think we are going the wrong way. We've crossed over into Kansas, and the address for the luncheon is Kansas City, Missouri."

"What! How could I be wrong?" I looked at the directions, but I guess I hadn't read them thoroughly. My mind became more clear.

"You know what, Kath? I just assumed the country club described to me on the phone was in Kansas. Since I thought I'd been there before, I figured I was going the right way. I guess I never really read the directions which were sent to me."

We had a good laugh, turned around at the next exit, and made the luncheon on time. What I assumed was forty-five minutes from our house was actually twenty. If I'd only read the directions!

Read the Directions.

Have you ever done that? Have you ever thought you were driving the right direction but came to find out you were going the wrong way? It's really sad when a map is right under the seat or the directions are lying next to you in the car. We're just sure we can find the restaurant or friend's house, so we certainly won't stop and ask someone, and we might not even look at a map. We can be so proud! It's a humbling thing to say we need directions, we don't have all the answers, and we make mistakes.

God wants us to get the most out of life. He wants us to go the right direction and find the ultimate destination of heaven. He wants us to enjoy the trip and not become weary and frustrated from consistently making bad decisions and wrong turns. Therefore, God gave us directions for life. All the directions we need to live an abundant, joyful life are in His Word. But we must read the directions.

Is it from God?

The Bible is an amazing book. Historically, the Bible is 66 books, composed by 41 human authors, and written over approximately 1,550 years. By the end of the third century A.D., the separate books and letters were put into one document as men and women recognized them to be one book, with one Author—God.[80]

Do we today actually believe the Bible is the Word of God? And if we do, how should it affect our lives? Back in 1989, American pollster George Gallup, Jr. states, "Americans revere the Bible—but, mostly, they don't read it. And because they don't read it, they have become a nation of biblical illiterates."[81] He goes on to explain,

> Four Americans in five believe the Bible is the literal or inspired word of God, and many of those who don't, still regard it as the basis for moral values and the rule of law.... But despite the large percentage of Americans who believe the Bible is the word of God, only one-third of Americans read it at least once a week - 15 percent read it daily.... This lack of Bible-reading explains why Americans know so little about the Bible that is the basis of the faith of most of them. For example, eight in ten Americans say they are Christians, but only four in ten know that Jesus, according to the Bible, delivered the Sermon on the Mount.[82]

Do you believe that 80 percent of the United States' population are truly believers in Jesus Christ? In a more recent survey, George Barna maintains that five-sixths of the U.S. call themselves "Christian."[83] I consider these statistics outrageous. The condition of the Church in the United States and our society would prove differently. Only a small percentage of people have experienced true spiritual change in their lives. Further, I question that 80 percent of our population truly believes the Bible is the Word of God. There must be some misunderstanding in the questionnaires. Barna reports that more than 4 out of 5 adults name the Bible as the most influential book in human history, but he also states, "Unfortunately, owning copies of the Bible and truly possessing the truths of Scripture are two different realities. Americans have taken physical ownership of the Book but have not taken spiritual ownership of its content. For instance, only 4 out of 10 adults even read the Bible during a typical week, other than when they are in church. Those who read the Bible spend an average of roughly one hour during the entire week reading the Scriptures.... Reading, studying and reflecting on-much less applying-God's Word is a highly regarded idea, but it's not a top priority for most people."[84]

At the beginning of each National Football League season, a professional football player receives a playbook. It's his job to study it and then carry out the duties assigned to him. If the player doesn't do this to the satisfaction of the coaching staff, he'll lose his job. The coach will hire someone who is willing to study the book and who can carry out the plays with the required consistency. If the player truly believes his livelihood depends on being a student of the playbook, he will study the book with all diligence. In many ways, his life depends on it.

The lack of Bible reading in our society and in the church is evidence that many aren't Christians as they claim to be. This neglect also shows that many people who say the Bible is the Word of God don't seriously believe it is. If the Bible is truly God's Word to us, then it's a greater treasure than the Hope diamond. It has more grandeur than the Rocky Mountains. It has more value than all the gold in Fort Knox.

So why do many treat the Bible as if it were a relic in a museum? We may look at it with feelings of nostalgia and mystery, but we allow it to collect dust on our shelves as we walk by it every day. If the Bible is truly the Word of God, then we should humbly cherish it as a man finding an oasis in the desert. It's water bringing life to our souls. We should lap it into our hearts as the deer who pants for water. Show me a person who *knows* the Bible is the Word of God, and I will show you a person who keeps his *nose* in the Book.

The Testimony of Jesus

We have many reasons to believe the Bible is truly the Word of God.[85] Jesus certainly affirmed the Bible was the Word of God, inspired by the Holy Spirit. He often quoted the Old Testament as the Word of God.[86] For Jesus, the Old Testament Scriptures were the authority for life. In Matthew 22:43, referring to Psalm 110:1, Jesus said, "Then how does David in the Spirit call Him 'Lord.'" Jesus acknowledged that the Holy Spirit of God spoke through David. In John 17:17, Jesus referred to God's Word, the Old Testament then, as the word of truth. Jesus knew the Old Testament was the authoritative Word of God.

The Testimony of Prophecies

We are well aware of prophecies concerning the initial coming of the Messiah that are fulfilled in Jesus of Nazareth.[87] But there are many other prophecies that have also been fulfilled in the Scriptures.

In Genesis 15:13-14, God told Abraham 600 years before its occurrence that His people would be slaves in a foreign land for 400 years. God also said they'd be delivered and come out of bondage with many possessions. We know from the Exodus Moses led the people out of Egypt after 430 years of bondage and that the Egyptians lavished gifts upon Israel as they left.

We also see God's voice in the prophecies of Isaiah, Jeremiah, and Micah. They prophesied to the southern kingdom of Judah that it would fall as the northern kingdom had fallen. As well, many prophets (i.e., Obadiah) spoke harshly against Edom and prophesied its annihilation. Today we can visit Petra in Edom — an easily defended city set in red clay, with its only entrance a long, narrow pathway through 100-foot cliffs. Yet the city is uninhabited. As with Judah, the Babylonians destroyed Edom.[88] Reading in Malachi 1:2-4, we find that near the middle of the fifth century, Edom was desolate.[89]

Another realized prophecy was Isaiah's prediction of Babylon's fall and Cyrus' coming at the height of the Babylonian regime.[90] Further, we know that Jeremiah's prophecy of the seventy-year captivity of Israel[91] was fulfilled in the rebuilding of the temple in 516 B.C.[92] Jesus predicted the fall of Jerusalem and the destruction of the temple.[93] Approximately thirty-seven years after His death, the Romans took it apart piece by piece. There are multifarious predictions that have already been fulfilled concerning the nations of the world and the people of God.[94] Only our omniscient God who knows the past, present, and future could write such prophecies. He spoke through men, but the words were His.

The Testimony of Scripture

The Word of God often came to prophets in the Old Testament era.[95] Also, the Word of the Lord is frequently spoken of in the New Testament.[96] Peter declared in 2 Peter 1:20-21, "But know this first of all, that no prophecy of Scripture is a matter of one's own interpretation, for no prophecy was ever made by an act of human will, but men moved by the Holy Spirit spoke from God." Paul claimed the inspiration of Scripture in 2 Timothy 3:16. He wrote, "All Scripture is inspired[97] by God."

Lest we think these verses refer only to the Old Testament, we find that the New Testament prophets recognized their inspiration. The apostle Paul stated this:

> Now we have received, not the spirit of the world, but the Spirit who is from God, that we might know the things freely given to us by God, which things we also speak, not in words taught by human wisdom, but in those taught by the Spirit, combining spiritual thoughts with spiritual words.[98]

The apostle Peter, referring to his inspired co-worker Paul, proclaimed in 2 Peter 3:15-16,

> ... and regard the patience of our Lord to be salvation; just as also our beloved brother Paul, according to the wisdom given him, wrote to you, as also in all his letters, speaking in them of these things, in which are some things hard to understand, which the untaught and unstable distort, as they do also the rest of the Scriptures, to their own destruction.

Here Peter equated Paul's letters with the rest of Scripture.

Yes, through Jesus' words, the prophecies fulfilled in Scripture, and the testimony of Scripture itself, we can firmly trust that the Bible is the very Word of God.

The Testimony of History

Throughout the history of Israel and the church, people have believed the Scriptures were the Word of God. Moses commanded the Levites to put the Book of the Law beside the ark of the covenant.[99] Later, during the reign of Josiah when Hilkiah found the Book of the Law, Josiah began a revival in the land out of humble reverence. Why? Because he found that God's people had been disobedient to God's Word.[100]

Jesus and the early church always believed the Old Testament Scriptures were God's Word. Bible scholar F.F. Bruce, in referring to the Lord and the apostles, said "... when they spoke of 'the scriptures' they knew which writings they had in mind and could distinguish them from other writings which were not included in 'the scriptures.'"[101] The church father Ignatius wrote in his letter to the Philadelphians (about 100 A.D.),

> Yet your prayers to God will make me perfect so that I may gain that fate which I have mercifully been allotted, by taking refuge in the "Gospel," as in Jesus' flesh, and in the "Apostles," as in the presbytery of the Church. And the "Prophets," let us love them too, because they anticipated the gospel in their preaching and hoped for and awaited Him, and were saved by believing on him.[102]

Ignatius likened the Gospels and the Epistles (the various letters of the New Testament written by the apostles), with the prophets in the Old Testament. The Swiss reformer John Calvin wrote in his famous Institutes,

> When that which is set forth is acknowledged to be the Word of God, there is no one so deplorably insolent—unless devoid also both of common sense and of humanity itself—as to dare impugn the credibility of Him who speaks.[103]

Mega-dittos, Brother John. John Calvin, of the sixteenth century, believed the Bible, as we know it, was the Word of God.

Throughout church history, most people haven't

questioned the authenticity of the Bible as God's Word. Only in the last two centuries have more than a few doubted the veracity of the Scriptures. These choose to depend on their own rationalism instead of a supernatural God who could and would intervene in history. However, if the claims of criticism and skepticism had any credence, we would have known it long ago.

Yes, a person can explain the Scriptures through hypothesis and critical theories which lead to disbelief, but certainly there is no reason that we *must* do so. If there was only one archeological find that disproved the Bible, it would be in every headline. But there isn't one. Archeologists continue to find data, like the Mari letters, the Nuzi tablets, and the scrolls of Qumran, which point to the reliability of Scripture.[104] Archeology and history continue to remind us we can fully trust the Bible as God's Word.

The Testimony of Changed Lives

Possibly the greatest evidence the Bible is the Word of God is the influence its words have had on millions of lives. The Bible says in Hebrews 4:12, "For the Word of God is living and active and sharper than any two-edged sword, and piercing as far as the division of soul and spirit, of both joint and marrow, able to judge the thoughts and intentions of the heart." The Holy Spirit will often use Scripture to convict people of their sin and need for Christ.

One such person from history is Saint Augustine. As Saint Augustine (430 d.) wept with sorrow concerning his sin, he heard a small voice say, "Take it and read, take it and read." Augustine obeyed. Quoting Romans 13:13 and 14, he had this life-changing response:

> 'Not in reveling and drunkenness, not in lust and wantonness, not in quarrels and rivalries.

> Rather, arm yourselves with the Lord Jesus Christ; spend no more thought on nature and nature's appetites.' I had no wish to read more and no need to do so. For in an instant, as I came to the end of the sentence, it was as though the light of confidence flooded into my heart and all the darkness of doubt was dispelled.[105]

During his study of the book of Romans, Martin Luther said,

> Then I grasped that the justice of God is that righteousness by which through grace and sheer mercy God justifies us through faith. Thereupon I felt myself to be reborn and to have gone through open doors into paradise.... This passage of Paul became to me a gate of heaven.[106]

Brother Andrew didn't understand why he hungered so to read the Bible. He had picked it up in his hospital room and couldn't put it down. Reading Scripture led him to pray, "Lord, if You will show me the way, I will follow you...." God did show him the way and used him mightily. Brother Andrew smuggled Bibles into the closed countries of eastern Europe.[107] The Bible changes lives, even as Scripture teaches, "So faith comes from hearing, and hearing by the word of Christ."[108]

Take it and Read

There's plenty of evidence to encourage believing the Bible is what it claims to be—the Word of God. We must, therefore, humble ourselves and read it. We must admit we need God's direction and commands for life. His Word is not the suggestion of a Sunday School teacher. It's not the opinion of a broadcaster. It's not an oracle by a philosopher. The Bible is God's Word to His beloved creatures, and we are to read it.

We are to read it because He commands us to read it. God tells us through Paul in Colossians 3:16, "Let the Word of Christ richly dwell within you." The words of our Lord will only take root in our hearts if we listen to them, read them, study them, memorize them, and meditate on them. Paul urged Timothy, "Be diligent to present yourself approved to God as a workman who doesn't need to be ashamed, handling accurately the word of truth" (2 Timothy 2:15).

I remember listening to my parents' Bill Cosby record album years ago. He jested you never want to hear your surgeon say "Oops!" as you went under. You want and expect your doctor to be accurate. He or she trained diligently for years to precisely treat your body. We must study the Word with even more diligence. Someday we'll stand before God and be held accountable for how we applied His Word to our lives.

There are no short cuts to precision training in the Word of God. I'm not saying every person must go to Bible college or seminary. Some of our finest Bible teachers didn't have formal education. But, if we want to be humble disciples of Jesus Christ, we must assiduously study the Word of God. We must spend much time and energy getting a grip on the Word of God so it can get a grip on us. God commanded Hebrew fathers to carry the Word on their hearts so they might teach the Word to their sons.[109] He told Joshua the Israelites were to meditate upon His words day and night.[110] There are copious verses reminding us of our heavenly Father's commands to know and study His Word.[111]

We should also read the Bible because it will be profitable for us. George Muller, of Bristol Orphanage fame in

England, and a man of exceedingly great faith, said, "Great has been the blessing from consecutive, diligent, daily study. I look upon it as a lost day when I have not had a good time over the Word of God."[112]

Most business people today work for profit-making organizations. Their biggest concern is, "How much are we going to put into our pockets at the end of the day?" In a 1993 issue, U.S. News and World Report did a cover story on Bill Gates, founder of Microsoft. At that time, nearly 90 percent of all personal computers used Microsoft operating systems. If you had invested $2,100 in Microsoft stock in 1986, in 1993, that stock would have been worth over $77,000.[113] That's a pretty hefty seven year return. Today, the value is about ten times that of 1993. Everyone would say that's a substantial profit. Bill Gates was reportedly worth over six billion dollars at the ripe old age of thirty-seven.

Many investors made thousands, if not millions, of dollars in the 1990s as the stock market sky-rocketed. What a profitable time to be in the market. Tragically for many, as the new millennium began, some technology stocks fell ninety percent or worse. Many who hoped for early retirement and fat pensions now need further employment.

God promises if we hide His Word in our hearts and walk in obedience to it, we'll have success and much profit. I'm not necessarily speaking of financial profit, but as we walk in the Spirit according to God's Word, He will fill our souls with peace and love. Listen to these promises from God:

> This book of the law shall not depart from your mouth but you shall meditate on it day and night, so that you may be careful to do according to all that is written in it; for then you will make your way prosperous, and then you will have success (Joshua 1:8).
>
> If you abide in My word, then you are truly

> disciples of Mine, and you shall know the truth and the truth will set you free (John 8:31-32).

If you want to know peace in your heart, if you want to know freedom from the snares of this world, you must get into the Word of God. A weekend drinking binge doesn't lead to happiness. Living with someone without the commitment of marriage only leads to mistrust and devaluation of self-worth. Being overly committed to the corporate pursuit eventually leaves loneliness and emptiness in the soul, not fulfillment. Sin destroys our lives, some more slowly than others. No sin brings true fulfillment. To find true joy we must walk the path of righteousness. That path is found in God's Word. "How can a young man keep His way pure? By keeping it according to Thy Word" (Psalm 119:9). The psalmist also states in Psalm 119:24, "Thy testimonies also are my delight; They are my counselors."

Finding Abundance

God wants to give us direction, purpose, and peace. But we can only find these and other fruits of abundance if we walk according to His Word. The Word of God is indeed profitable for our lives. Paul reminded Timothy, "All Scripture is inspired by God and profitable for teaching, for reproof, for correction, for training in righteousness, that the man of God may be adequate, equipped for every good work" (2 Timothy 3:16-17). The best investment you can make is spending at least fifteen minutes a day reading the Book of Life, God's Word.[114] God has the answers to life and we don't. If we are going to live in abundance, we must live in humility according to His Word.

If you've never tried to read the Bible on your own, I encourage you to begin in the gospel of John. There we find a beautiful portrait of our Savior, written by His beloved disciple. Then maybe read a few of the shorter epistles in the New Testament, like Philippians or 1 John. Make it your goal to read at least one chapter of the Bible each day. Feel free to use a modern translation like the New International Version or the New American Standard. Paraphrases like The Living Bible or The Message can be especially helpful to the new believer. There are many good translations, just make sure you are getting into the Book.

I also recommend joining a Bible Study group as soon as possible. You can gain encouragement there and rub shoulders with those who can help you learn how to study Scripture effectively. As well, make sure you are attending a church that firmly believes and applies the truth that the Bible is God's Word. Many churches today are being conformed to the world because they don't hold to the infallible and inerrant Word of God.

God has given us the directions for life. They are in His Word. Yet for many of us His Word is still on the shelf. For others we only open His plan for us on Sunday mornings. If we choose not to humble ourselves and submit to His Word, we'll go the wrong direction. We'll follow the world when our destination was walking with God.

Don't find out the hard way. Don't wait until you become totally frustrated. Open your Bible now. As you read with a humble heart, God will show you direction for life.

A Suggested Prayer:

Gracious Lord and Author of Life, I thank You for revealing Your will for my life through Your Holy Book, the Bible. Forgive me for not reading, studying and applying it as I should. Help me through discipline, humility and love to read Your Word daily. Please use Your Word to transform my life that I might be a vessel of honor who glorifies You. In Jesus' name, Amen.

Chapter 7

The Dependence of Humility

A young boy, ready for bed, interrupted a family gathering in the living room. "I'm going up to say my prayers now. Anybody want anything?"[115]

For many, prayer is just a way to ask their heavenly sugar daddy to grant them prosperity and perks. If they are in a fix, they talk to Mr. Fix-It, but otherwise they depend upon themselves and the world. We pray the prayer of Jabez (1 Chronicles 4:10) when we need protection, or want to increase our success in the business world, but we don't talk with the Lord just to spend time with Him. Don't get me wrong. God wants to hear and meet our needs according to His perfect timing and will, but prayer is to be much more than just asking and receiving.

A Love Relationship

First and foremost, "Prayer is the acid test of devotion."[116] One of the greatest ways you can tell people are in love is how often they talk with one another. When I was engaged to Kathy (who is now my wife), I wanted to communicate with her daily. I wanted to share my heart and my feelings with her. I wanted to know her, and I wanted her to know me.

Ours was mainly a long distance relationship. While I studied at seminary near Chicago, she took courses at the University of Kansas. With an eleven-hour drive separating us, weekend trips were out. Most of our relationship had to be developed via phone calls and letters. Due to cost, we couldn't talk on the phone as often as we would have liked. We also had to limit our discussions and whisperings on the telephone to about thirty minutes. I wrote Kathy a letter almost daily. Sometimes she received two letters in her sorority mail box on the same day. I often received letters as well.

Why did we communicate so much? Because we were desperately, passionately in love. We wanted oneness in our lives. Emotional, physical, spiritual oneness, and therefore we got married. People in love want and need to communicate with one another. Now one of the best ways I can show Kathy I love and appreciate her is to sit and talk with her, listen to her emotions and the details of her day. It's also essential I share my feelings with her (which I often do poorly). Communication is vital in any growing relationship.

Real Devotion

When we pray we are showing God we love, trust, and need Him. As I mentioned previously, we show God we love Him through our obedience.[117] The first step in our obedience and devotion to God is prayer.[118]

We see this in the life of Jesus. No one will ever love the Father as much as His Son, Jesus. An outstanding evidence of His love for His Father is the priority that Jesus placed upon prayer. I have often thought that Jesus prayed so much because He had to make so many critical decisions. Certainly these decisions weighed heavily in His need to pray. Yet, I believe that Jesus also prayed much because He enjoyed it. He loved His Father and therefore, Jesus wanted to speak with Him.

Luke 5:16 states, "But He Himself would often slip away to the wilderness and pray." Jesus missed the constant fellowship with the Father He had known since eternity past. He used these often late night or early morning sessions to share His heart and His experiences with the One He loved so very much.

Jesus had every excuse not to pray. As the Son of God, didn't He already know the will of the Father? Why did He need to convene with God if He was always full of His Spirit?[119] He also could have used exhaustion as an excuse to not pray. Mark 1:34 describes Jesus spending much time and energy ministering to the needs of people. Battling in spiritual warfare, such as casting out demons, must have been physically and emotionally draining. He must have been worn to a frazzle. But Jesus got up early the next morning to spend essential time with the Father. Jesus arose before daylight, sometime between 3:00 a.m. and 6:00 a.m., so He could get His day started right.[120] It sounds like an engaged couple meeting early in the morning for breakfast before they go to work. They can't wait until dinner to see one another because they are enthralled, mesmerized, and captivated by the other person's presence. Jesus thrived on the prayerful presence of the Father. He knew as no other, "In Thy presence is fullness of joy, and in Thy right hand there are treasures forever."[121]

As we come to God in prayer we show Him our devotion and love. As well, we find His love for us. A wonderful thing about spending time in the presence of God is that we know He will always listen. No matter what we've done, what questions we have, or how tongue tied we get, He will always listen. He is waiting for us with open arms to hold and cherish us. God tells us in Isaiah 40:11, "Like a shepherd He will tend His flock, in His arm He will gather the lambs, and carry them in His bosom...."

When we come to God in prayer, we need not fear rejection, embarrassment, or condemnation. God isn't our earthly father who failed us. He's not our former husband who degraded us. He accepts us as we are, with all of our flaws and scars. There is no need to go to the salon before we meet with God because we are clothed with the robe of His righteousness. We can come to His throne of grace and mercy boldly through Jesus Christ.[122] Our sin and guilt were paid at Calvary. Once we receive His payment for us, we become sons and daughters of God, and God will not reject us.[123] We can cry out to the throne, "Abba, Father," and our beloved Dad will treasure that term of endearment.

Then, as we come before Him recognizing His love, recognizing His mercy, recognizing His benevolence toward us, we will want to tell Him how much we love Him. We will want to share our hearts with Him, and willingly become vulnerable to our Heavenly Father. As we open our lives and display our broken hearts, we will weep with joy and sorrow in His presence. How will God respond? Will He judge us? Will He bring His wrath against us? Will He laugh at us? No. We are His children—His own possession.[124] He will fill us with comfort, hold us in His arms, and whisper through the Spirit in our hearts, "I love you. Please tell me more. I want to listen."

Further, as He puts balm on our wounds and fills our hearts with the joy of His presence, we will learn to respond to Him with words of love and devotion. We will learn He truly is our confidante, our best friend, and our beloved. Being naked and vulnerable before Him will no longer make us feel like hiding. Our fellowship with Him will be as close as we can come today to what Adam and Eve experienced with God in Eden prior to sin.

Let us come to God in prayer and give Him pleasure as we respond in faith to His love for us. Proverbs 15:8 says, "The sacrifice of the wicked is an abomination to the

LORD, but the prayer of the upright is His delight." What an amazing thing that as we show God our devotion through prayer, we bring delight to His heart.[125]

In Times of Crises

Prayer is not only the test of our devotion to God. Prayer is also the test of our dependence upon God. When do you hear about prayer in our society? Usually, we only hear about prayer through the secular media when there is a crisis. Why? Because in times of crises, people recognize they can no longer depend upon themselves, other people, or the braces of this world.

You may recall in the 9-11 tragedy how often the news media talked about people praying for the victims and their families. It was a time of crisis. It was a time when life and death issues were at hand, and therefore people recognized their limitations and turned to a Supreme Being. President Bush rightly called for a National Day of Prayer on September 14, 2001 to help us mourn and encourage one another during this calamity.

At the beginning of the Gulf War in 1992, General Norman Schwarzkopf wrote this to his family:

> Some will die; many could die. I pray to God that this will not happen but if it does and if I am one of those chosen by God to sacrifice my life, I wanted you to know that my last thoughts before this terrible beginning are of you, my beloved family.[126]

In times of crises we turn to prayer. I heard the radio report of some lost skiers in Colorado being rescued after five days. The reporter introduced the story saying "many prayers have been answered." Alcoholics Anonymous, with its Christian foundations, discusses the need to depend upon a Higher Power and to seek help from Him. When we are at the end of our rope and there is nothing else we can do, many of us gain comfort in talking with someone greater than ourselves who may be able to sovereignly fix the situation. Many do this even when they don't fully understand Who that Higher Power is.[127] Respected researcher George Barna writes, "Millions of adults say they believe in and worship God, but they have no idea what worship means, who God is, what He stands for or what He expects of those who wish to relate to Him."[128]

As Christians, we know The Power. We recognize that God often uses times of crises to draw us closer to Him. We learn dependence upon God when our circumstances are out of our control. We are humbled, because we are limited, and therefore we look to God.

Responding with Prayer

The early church depended upon God when it could have been easily wiped out. Their leader had been killed.[129] They were outcasts from their Jewish heritage. They were being persecuted by the Romans. How did they respond? Prayer.

In Luke 24:49, Jesus commanded the believers to stay in the city and wait for the coming of the Holy Spirit. Immediately, after the ascension of Jesus in Acts 1:9-11, the apostles and believers returned to Jerusalem from Mount Olivet and gathered in the upper room. What was their mission? Prayer. Acts 1:14 declares, "These all with one mind were continually devoting themselves to prayer,...." They humbly depended on God and sought His will through prayer.

Jesus commanded them to wait, and wait they did. Seven days later[130] we find them still in the upper room, and still waiting for the coming of the Spirit. The apostles and the Church knew they had no power in themselves. All the apostles had failed Jesus when He needed them most. They didn't want to fail their Savior again, so they waited upon God in prayer.

God was faithful as always. At Pentecost, He filled them with the power of His Holy Spirit so they could be witnesses of the resurrection power of Jesus Christ to the world. After this miraculous event, their dependence upon God grew. Spiritual pride could have taken hold when about three thousand souls were saved. But the church further submitted to God by continual devotion to prayer.[131] They were in full and complete dependence upon God and His leading.

On My Knees

During the early stages of beginning a local church I learned much about depending upon the Lord. My wife and I answered the call of God and the Evangelical Free Church to start a local church in Lee's Summit, Missouri (a suburb of Kansas City). At the outset, we knew no one there. When we accepted the call to go, we had no financial support other than our savings, which would only last a few months. We felt very much on our own, but God was near. I found myself often on my knees, seeking God's will. Asking for His vision. Asking for our daily bread.

During this time I drew heavily upon the faithfulness of God in His Word and in the lives of men like C.T. Studd, George Muller, and David Brainerd. These men also ventured out in faith, put their lives on the line, and learned to trust God. Indeed, during crises we learn more about trusting Him. I leaned upon the familiar promises of Matthew 6:33, Philippians 4:19, and Proverbs 3:5-6. I had memorized these verses in previous years, but now they took on real significance.

As Kathy and I stepped out in faith, God drew us near to Himself and began to reveal His love and plan for us. Supernaturally, He arranged for us within the first month of our endeavor to meet four families who became involved in the leadership of our church. Wonderfully, God supplied seed money for this mission through our home church in Barrington, Illinois and through a church planting grant I received through Trinity Evangelical Divinity School. Within four months, the new church families were paying my base salary.

Yes, in times of crises we learn to trust God. In times of crises we learn to depend upon God. In times of crises prayer becomes real, and hopefully God becomes real to us.

Responding to Crises

We can respond to crises in one of two ways. We can blame God, or thank God. If we blame God, we create bitterness and hatred, fleeing from the One who can help us and love us the most. If we have a tantrum while we are drowning, our rescuer won't be able to grab on. Let us rest in our Father's arms. We must believe God truly does work all things to the good, to those who love Him and are called according to His purpose (Romans 8:28). We must allow God to use crises in our lives as fire perfecting gold, as the trainer pushing the athlete through pain to win the race. God is conforming us to the image of His Son[132] as the potter working with clay.[133] Therefore, let us pray in crises and allow God to pour the water of His Spirit on our souls so we might be pliable in His hands.[134]

It's always Time to Pray

However, God is not just a God for times of crises. We miss true abundance in prayer and in our walk with

God if we don't constantly seek Him. Any time we aren't consistently pouring out our hearts to God in prayer, we are walking in pride. A lack of prayer says to God, out of the vile nature of our hearts, "I can do it myself." In Chapter 2, we defined sin as *arrogant disobedience to God*. Pride is *arrogance toward God*, since pride is the beginning attitude of sin.

One of the greatest forms of pride today, even in the church, is prayerlessness. We have learned to lean upon our programs and strategies rather than upon God. The Wednesday night prayer service has been replaced with fund-raising programs. Early morning times of supplication have been replaced by church growth strategies.[135] As one author said, "Prayer is where the action is. Any church without a well-organized and systematic prayer program is simply operating a religious treadmill."[136]

Just as we have churches with large programs and no power, we have many Christians with busy schedules and no power. A humble person must be a person of prayer. E.M. Bounds, author of many classics concerning prayer, wrote, "The man—God's man—is made in the closet."[137] That is why Paul exhorted us to "Pray without ceasing" (1 Thessalonians 5:17). He admonished in Colossians 4:2, "Devote yourselves to prayer, keeping alert in it with an attitude of thanksgiving." Our devotion to prayer shows our devotion to and dependence upon God. The most humbling position in the world is on our knees before God in prayer with open hearts.

The Glory of His Presence

As we come into His presence, we see His glory and recognize our inadequacies and sinfulness. Isaiah cowered before God as he experienced God's holiness.[138] The glory of Almighty God floored Saul of Tarsus.[139] In the book of

Revelation, our Lord's presence dropped John as a dead man.[140] These men saw God and fell at His feet.

Why do so many of us fail to consistently go before God's throne? Why do we often go through the motions of praying rather than seeking the presence of God? We're afraid we'll be found out. We're afraid to see ourselves as we truly are. We're ashamed and embarrassed by our lack of holiness. Compared to God we are but filthy rags.[141]

But in Christ, we need not fret. In Him, we are righteous,[142] clothed with His garments. We must humbly recognize we are lost without Him, and therefore we must depend upon Him all the more for every detail of our lives. He is our Sustainer who knows the future and has all power. He is the One who can do all wonders.[143] Let us therefore lift every need of every moment into His glorious hands. Let us start every day telling Him not only that we love Him, but that we depend upon Him. Let us declare our allegiance to Him as our Master and Lord. Each day, let us ask Him to live and work through us in the power of His Holy Spirit.

Starting each day with the Lord renews our commitment to Him. It says we truly believe He is in control and there is enough time in the day to accomplish all He wants done. There is enough time in every day, no matter what your schedule, to spend time with your Beloved <u>and</u> do a good job at work and home.

Do you believe if you committed twenty minutes each day to the Word and prayer, God would give you back that time and more in wisdom and joy? Many people believe it's a wise time investment to plan their schedules on detailed planners or PDAs. Yet these same people find it hard to believe the Author of time will multiply their hours if they put Him first. We lack wisdom at work because we don't ask.[144] We lack patience at home because we don't pray.[145] God will provide all of our needs, but we must put Him first.[146] Andrew Bonar, a Scottish pastor of the nineteenth century, said, "By the grace of God and the strength of His Holy Spirit I desire to lay down the rule not to speak to man until I have spoken to God: not to do anything with my hand until I have been upon my knees...."[147]

Put God first in your day. Don't give Him the leftovers. Too often we ask Him to bless decisions we've already made on our own. That leads to humiliation and a waste of energy and time. Let us humble ourselves in dependence upon God and seek Him first no matter what the need and no matter what the moment.[148] He will give you peace, even when your schedule is busy. He will fill you with joy, even when the circumstances surrounding you are dismal.

Commence Prayer

The story is told of an airliner bound for New York in 1986. It began as the kind of flights most of us like—uneventful. But this soon changed. Descending to the destination, the pilot realized the landing gear refused to engage. He worked the controls back and forth, trying again and again to lock the gear into place. No success. He then asked the control tower for instructions as he circled the landing field. Responding to the crisis, airport personnel sprayed the runway with foam as fire trucks and other emergency vehicles moved into position. Disaster hovered minutes away. The passengers, meanwhile, were told of each maneuver in that calm, cheery voice pilots manage to use at times like this. Flight attendants glided about the cabin with an air of cool reserve. Passengers received instructions to place their heads between their knees and grab their ankles just before impact. It was one of those "I can't believe this is happening to me" experiences. There were tears and a few screams of despair in the last seconds before landing. Suddenly the pilot announced over the intercom, "We are beginning our final descent. At this moment, in accordance with International Aviation Codes established at

Geneva, it's my obligation to inform you that if you believe in God you should commence prayer."

The belly landing occurred without a hitch. No one was injured and, aside from some rather extensive damage to the plane, the airline hardly remembered the incident. A relative of one of the passengers called the airline the very next day and asked about the prayer rule the pilot had quoted. No one volunteered any information on the subject. They said coolly, "No comment."[149]

Humble yourselves before God in prayer. Our prayers show Him our devotion to Him. Our prayers show God our dependence upon Him. Tonight when you get on your knees before bed, don't just call in a request list to a heavenly sugar daddy. Tell Your Father you love Him and that you want to live your life in humble dependence upon Him.

A Suggested Prayer:

Oh, Lord, make me a person of prayer. Give me a heart to cry out to You for all my needs and desires. I fully and completely depend upon You for every aspect of my life. Let Your Spirit not only teach me how to pray, but stir my soul so that I would daily pray Your will for Your glory. In Jesus name, Amen.

Chapter 8

The Love of Humility

According to one legend, Valentine was an early Christian who made friends with many children. He enjoyed their company and companionship. However the Romans imprisoned him because he refused to worship their various gods. Valentine's imprisonment upset his young friends. They longed to tell him of their affection, so they tossed notes of love through his cell window bars. That is how valentines began. On Valentine's Day, people of all ages remember those they love by sending valentine messages of affection and friendship.[150]

God sent us a valentine. He loved us so much He sent His Son to die and pay for our sins. Since God loved us that much, we ought to love one another. The disciple whom Jesus loved wrote,

> Beloved, let us love one another, for love is from God; and everyone who loves is born of God and knows God. The one who does not love does not know God, for God is love. By this the love of God was manifested in us, that God has sent His only begotten Son into the world so that we

> might live through Him. In this is love, not that we loved God, but that He loved us and sent His Son to be the propitiation for our sins. Beloved, if God so loved us, we also ought to love one another (1 John 4:7-11).

Since God has loved us so much through His Son, how should we respond?

Responding in Obedience

I remember thinking how fantastic it is that God sent His Son to die on the cross for me. I contemplated many ways to show God my heart for Him. These ranged from writing God a love-letter to selling all my possessions and becoming an itinerant evangelist preaching on street corners.

If we love God, we want to please Him. Because His love for us is so extraordinary, we want to do extraordinary things for Him. And yet, as I pondered this concept of loving God, a verse came to mind which described the best way to show God my heart for Him. John 14:21 says, "He who has My commandments and keeps them, he it is who loves Me; and he who loves Me shall be loved by My Father, and I will love him, and disclose Myself to him." That is what God wanted. He simply wanted me to obey Him. "To obey is better than sacrifice."[151] There was nothing extraordinary I needed to do to display my love for God. He only wanted my obedience.

Most women enjoy the special gifts their husbands purchase for them on birthdays. Cards, flowers, chocolates, or other special gifts can show someone love. Imagine how a wife feels when her birthday is the only time her husband does anything for her. When she asks him to take out the trash, he keeeps watching the football game. When she asks him to help with the dishes, he keeps surfing the net. When she asks him to rub her back, he tells her he's too tired. He never takes her out to eat nor listens to her share about the challenges of her day. When he comes home from work, he turns on the television, expects dinner, and wants to be left alone.

How much do you think a box of chocolates on her birthday is going to mean? *Relationships depend upon consistent, meaningful experiences, not upon one-time events.* To develop a true love-relationship with our spouses, we must work hard at the relationship and respond to their needs and wants throughout the year.

It's the same in our relationship with God. We can't buy God's love through attending church once a week. We can't earn God's favor through writing an offering check once a month. What does it say to God when we shove down a quick devotional before bed after spending an hour watching CNN?

We show God how much we love and appreciate Him through a consistent effort to obey the commands of His Word. Throughout Scripture we find this truth.

> If you love Me, you will keep My commandments (John 14:15).
>
> If you keep My commandments, you will abide in My love; just as I have kept My Father's commandments, and abide in His love (John 15:10).
>
> For this is the love of God, that we keep His commandments; and His commandments are not burdensome (1 John 5:3).
>
> And this is love, that we walk according to His commandments. This is the commandment, just as you have heard from the beginning, that you should walk in it (2 John 1:6).

It's bogus to say we truly love God when we don't

humble our lives before Him in submissive obedience. Quite often in Scripture, loving God is paralleled with observing His commandments. One example is found in Exodus 20:6, "but showing lovingkindness to thousands, to those who love Me and keep My commandments."[152]

Therefore, to love God truly, we must first know His commands. We must have His commands in our heads and hearts. We do this by saturating ourselves with His Word. The Word of God tells us how to respond and obey in multifarious situations. The Word of God renews our minds so we'll be conformed to the image of Christ and not to the image of the world.[153] If you really want to show God how much you love Him, you must partake of His Word. Then, after you study it, you must submit humbly to it and obey. That's truly loving God.

It's a great joy when my children carry out their weekly responsibilities of taking out the trash and washing dishes. It means they are maturing and understanding responsibility. But as well, it means they're growing in respect and love for me. I'm the one who asked them to do these tasks. If they choose not to obey, they are saying they don't love me and respect my authority in their lives. In the same way, our humble obedience shows God we love and respect Him. It will put a smile on His face every time.

Responding with Love to Others

As we love God and follow His commands, we will also love others. "By this we know that we love the children of God, when we love God and observe His commandments" (1 John 5:2). The Bible gives us insight into how we can love and relate to others. The subject could be a two-volume book all by itself,[154] but let us glimpse at how, by knowing God's Word and submitting to it, we can learn to love others.

The Golden Rule. Growing up, one of the key principles in our home was the Golden Rule, "Do unto others as you would have others do unto you." For many years, I assumed the Golden Rule was like "cleanliness is next to godliness," a cliché that many assume is in the Bible, but is not. However, the Golden Rule is in the Bible. Jesus declared in Matthew 7:12, "Therefore, however you want people to treat you, so treat them, for this is the Law and the Prophets."

If we live by this principle, we will please God. If you wish others would listen to you, take time to listen to them. If you wish people would let you cut in line at the grocery store when you only have one item, let them go in front of you likewise. If you'd like your boss to commend your good work, make sure you encourage others when they do a good job. "Do unto others as you would have others do unto you." What a simple, yet profound, way to love people and humbly obey God. I hope my wife and I will consistently remind our children of this precept.

Sacrificial love. The ultimate principle in loving others is found in 1 John 3:16, "We know love by this, that He laid down His life for us; and we ought to lay down our lives for the brethren." We are to sacrifice, or deny ourselves, for other people. In our own strength, there is no way we can live out this statement. But as we submit our lives to God, and walk in the power of the Holy Spirit, He will enable us to live a life of sacrifice and service.

This principle can be applied in many ways. Philippians 2:3-4 lists ways we can humbly sacrifice for others. Remember the example of humility Jesus portrayed in Philippians 2:5-8? The Apostle Paul referred to this example when he wrote, "Do nothing from selfishness or empty conceit, but with humility of mind let each of you regard one another as more important than himself; do not merely look out for your own personal interests, but also for the interests of others." This is the "I am third" life, with God and others before ourselves. This is truly sacrificing for others.

As Cardinal Wolsey says to Lord Cromwell in Shakespeare's Henry VIII (Act III, Scene II, Line 441),

Cromwell, I charge thee, fling away ambition:
By that sin fell the angels. How can man then,
the image of his Maker, hope to win by't?
Love thyself last; cherish those hearts that hate thee;
Corruption wins not more than honesty.
Still in thy right hand carry gentle peace
To silence envious tongues. Be just, and fear not;
Let all the ends thou aim'st at be thy country's,
Thy God's, and truth's; then if thou fall'st, O Cromwell,
Thou fall'st a blessed martyr![155]

God must be our ultimate and first love. We must fling away ambition. We must put others before ourselves. After that, we can be concerned for our own needs. This is the crucified life.

The crucified father thinks, "I'd love to sleep in this Saturday morning, but it's the only extended time I'll have with my children this week. It's time to get up." The crucified husband considers, "Even though I want to relax after work, I know my wife also needs a break. I'll do the dishes tonight. Maybe we can relax together later."

The crucified friend says, "I know my own child is tough to handle, but I will invite Peggy's two boys over so she can get some shopping done."

The crucified church member ponders, "I think it would encourage Pastor George if I went to prayer meeting tonight. I'm going to skip my television watching and go. It would be good for my commitment to Christ as well."

God has not called us to love Him and others by discarding our own needs and desires. There will be times when we must have relaxation. There is nothing wrong with a few hours each week exercising, reading, or doing a hobby. But do we consistently put others before ourselves, or do we hoard our time and energy for things we want? We are to love others through sacrifice.

Forgiveness. Another way we can respond to God's love is by forgiving others. Again, Christ is our example in forgiving others. Paul says in Ephesians 4:29, "And be kind to one another, tender-hearted, forgiving each other, just as God in Christ also has forgiven you." He declared to the church at Colossae:

> And so, as those who have been chosen of God, holy and beloved, put on a heart of compassion, kindness, humility, gentleness and patience; bearing with one another, and forgiving each other, whoever has a complaint against anyone; just as the Lord forgave you, so also should you.[156]

I will leave the totality of these excellent passages for your further study and application. Our focus here is that we are to love others through forgiving them, whatever the hurt or pain, just as Christ has forgiven us. Just as we are not worthy of God's forgiveness, the parent who constantly called you stupid doesn't deserve your forgiveness. However, as God offers His forgiveness to anyone, we also should offer our forgiveness to anyone who has hurt or devastated us. If we are unwilling to forgive others, we are showing we have misunderstood the mercy and grace of God.

Jesus explained this in Matthew 18:21-35. Peter asked Him, "How often shall my brother sin against me and I forgive him?" Jesus replied we should continue to forgive the person no matter how many times he sins against us. Jesus told Peter and the disciples a parable about a king who forgave his slave an astronomical debt. In today's calculations, the slave owed the king over ten million dollars. Yet because of the slave's plea to the king, the king granted forgiveness. Then, in spite of the king's mercy, the slave demanded payment from a fellow slave who owed him about three months salary. What a pittance compared to the first slave's debt! Although the fellow slave begged for mercy, the ungrateful slave had him thrown into jail. When the king heard of this, he rebuked his slave for being unmerciful. Since the slave was unwilling to forgive those who owed him, the king had the unforgiving slave tortured. Jesus ended this parable by declaring, "So shall My heavenly Father also do to you, if each of you doesn't forgive his brother from your heart."

In the Lord's prayer in Matthew 6:12, Jesus taught us to pray, "And forgive us our debts, as we also have forgiven our debtors." If we are unwilling to forgive, this is a very scary prayer. Do we fully realize what we are asking God? If we knowingly harbor unforgiveness in our hearts, we are asking God not to forgive us. If we are to love others in obedience to God's Word, we must submit ourselves to His authority and forgive others no matter what they have done against us. We may not feel like forgiving, but if we truly understand what God has done for us, we will humbly seek to forgive others and not hold bitterness in our hearts.[157]

Dolly Madison, wife of James Madison, the United States' fourth president, was one of the most popular women in American history. Wherever she went, she charmed and captivated everyone, whether obscure or well-known, rich or poor, man or woman. Someone asked the secret of her power over others. Surprised by the question, Mrs. Madison exclaimed, "Power over people? I have none. I desire none. I merely love everyone."[158]

When we begin to love people according to the Word

of God, God will bless our relationships. Our hearts and lives will be filled with the joy of His Spirit. As well, people around us will be attracted to the love of Christ shining through us as we walk in the power of the Holy Spirit.

Our Valentine to God

In her Sonnets From the Portuguese, Elizabeth Barrett Browning asks the question, "How do I love Thee? Let me count the ways." Browning goes on to articulate,

> I love thee to the depth and breadth and height
> my soul can reach, when feeling out of sight
> for the ends of Being and ideal Grace.
> I love thee to the level of every day's
> most quiet need, by sun and candlelight.
> I love thee freely, as men strive for Right;
> I love thee purely, as they turn from Praise.
> I love thee with the passion put to use
> in my old griefs, and with my childhood's faith.
> I love thee with a love I seemed to lose
> with my lost saints,—I love thee with the breath,
> smiles, tears, of all my life!—and, if God choose,
> I shall but love thee better after death.[159]

My friends, let this sonnet be our valentine to God. By grateful obedience and loving others, we show our Father true love.

A Suggested Prayer:

My Loving Father, I can never repay all You have done for me through Jesus and the many blessings in my life. However, I do want to respond to Your love. I want to show

You with all my heart that I love You. Help me obey Your Word and be gracious to others as an act of devotion to You. In Jesus name, Amen.

Chapter 9

The Mandate of Humility

In Peters and Waterman's classic book on management, In Search of Excellence, one of the organizational principles they stress is that "excellent companies focus on only a few key business values, and a few objectives.[160] They further state,

> Let us suppose that we were asked for one all-purpose bit of advice for management, one truth that we were able to distill from the excellent companies research. We might be tempted to reply, "Figure out your value system. Decide what your company stands for. What does your enterprise do that gives everyone the most pride? Put yourself out ten or twenty years in the future: what would you look back on with greatest satisfaction?"[161]

Thomas Watson, Jr. of IBM fame, wrote in his book, A Business and Its Beliefs,

> I firmly believe that any organization, in order to survive and achieve success, must have a sound set of beliefs on which it premises all its policies and actions. Next, I believe that the most important single factor in corporate success is faithful adherence to those beliefs. And, finally, I believe if an organization is to meet the challenge of a changing world, it must be prepared to change everything about itself except those beliefs as it moves through corporate life.[162]

What are the beliefs of the church? What is the greatest value or mandate that Jesus left for His church? After the Great Commandment is the Great Commission.[163] The most familiar version of His mandate to the church is found in Matthew 28:18-20.[164]

> And Jesus came up and spoke to them, saying, "All authority has been given to Me in heaven and on earth. Go therefore and make disciples of all the nations, baptizing them in the name of the Father and the Son and the Holy Spirit, teaching them to observe all that I commanded you; and lo, I am with you always, even to the end of the age."

This charge is not an option. Our General has given our marching orders. He has given His plan to defeat the enemy, but now His troops must carry out the plan. Therefore, the submissive, humble disciple will help fulfill the Great Commission. There are three aspects to our involvement in the Great Commission.

Sharing our Faith

The first step in making disciples is sharing the good news of the gospel with those who need the Savior. This requires love, sensitivity, and dependence on the Holy Spirit. Discipleship authority Bill Hull has written, "If discipleship doesn't include evangelism, it doesn't deserve the name discipleship."[165]

The first word of Jesus in the Great Commission is "go." As we move throughout our lives, we are to share the love and message of the gospel with those around us. Jesus came to seek and to save the lost.[166] He left His throne in heaven to seek out those who needed His salvation. He is the Shepherd looking for the lost sheep. He is the woman looking for the lost coin. He is the Father anticipating the arrival of his prodigal son.[167] For too long, churches and individuals have viewed evangelism as an option, something only for the gifted or for the professional Christian. It's not.

Evangelism is a very humbling activity for those of us who believe we lack the gift of evangelism.[168] We shy away from verbally proclaiming the gospel. We've been inundated with the idea we shouldn't talk about God and politics in public, so we don't. We don't want to be embarrassed or cause a fuss.

My family attended a Halloween block party one fall before the presidential elections. Our kids presented themselves dressed in their full regalia of Halloween garb, whereas I think I wore a cowboy hat. Parties such as these are not my specialty. We didn't know many people. As the conversation progressed, someone brought up the upcoming election- who they were going to vote for, and why. Almost immediately, another person stated forcefully that we should not talk about religion or politics in public groups where someone might be offended. I immediately thought these are the very things we should talk about. Elections are extremely important to us, and things eternal are matters of life and death. These are the issues we should talk about, not the weather or how our favorite ball teams are playing. The eternal consequences and command of Christ demand we create and look for opportunities to share the gospel.

Eternal Consequences

The Bible is clear concerning the eternal destiny of those who die without knowing Christ personally.[169] Without Christ, each person will spend eternity away from the presence of God, without joy, peace, or love, in a fiery hell. From his classic book about revival, Why Revival Tarries, British evangelist Leonard Ravenhill told this story of a condemned man, Charlie Peace.

> Charlie Peace was a criminal. Laws of God or man curbed him not. Finally the law caught up with him, and he was condemned to death. On the fatal morning in Armley jail, Leeds, England, he was taken on the death-walk. Before him went the prison chaplain, routinely and sleepily reading some Bible verses. The criminal touched the preacher and asked what he was reading. "The Consolations of Religion," was the reply. Charlie Peace was shocked at the way he professionally read about hell. Could a man be so unmoved under the very shadow of the scaffold as to lead a fellow-human there and yet, dry-eyed, read of a pit that has no bottom into which this fellow must fall? Could this preacher believe the words that there is an eternal fire that never consumes its victims, and yet slide over the phrase

> without a tremor? Is a man human at all who can say with no tears, "You will be eternally dying and yet never know the relief that death brings?" All this was too much for Charlie Peace. So he preached. Listen to his on-the-eve-of-hell sermon. "Sir," addressing the preacher, "if I believed what you and the church of God say that you believe, even if England were covered with broken glass from coast to coast, I would walk over it, if need be, on hands and knees and think it worth while living, just to save one soul from an eternal hell like that!"[170]

We must be about God's business of urgently proclaiming the gospel because eternal souls are at stake.

The Urgency of the Gospel

I had just had a disheartening conversation with a building inspector who had come to check out our new church facility. We had to make some changes. He had almost shut us down. I was glad Randy, the deacon who oversaw our building, was there that afternoon. We consoled one another.

Then a man drove up in a white van. Randy and I went out to meet him, and he introduced himself as Ken. He had come to give us an estimate on putting up a sign for our church building. Quickly, we recognized Ken was a nice fellow who liked to talk. Seemingly on auto-pilot, with my spirit downcast from our run-in with the inspector, I attempted to share the gospel with Ken. I asked, "If you were to die tonight, do you think you'd go to heaven?" Ken wasn't sure. I told him he could find out through the Bible whether or not he would go to heaven.

In a somewhat hurried fashion, Ken and I went through the gospel tract The Four Spiritual Laws, with Randy looking on. Ken knew he wasn't a Christian, though he was familiar with what I shared. When we came to the point in the booklet which asked, "Would you like to receive Christ right now?" Ken said yes. Though I had done an unenthusiastic job of presenting the gospel, he was ready! Out in the parking lot, Ken bowed his head and prayed to receive Jesus as His Savior. I then told Ken that if he had sincerely asked Christ into his heart, he never needed to doubt again whether or not he'd go to heaven. Ken said, "If I hadn't been sincere, I wouldn't have prayed."

We explained to Ken the importance of getting involved with a local church. Since he lived on the other side of the metropolitan area, we recommended a couple of churches and then told him we would look forward to seeing him again in a couple of weeks when he came to put up our sign. Randy and I were amazed. God took us from one emotional extreme to the other. God turned our disappointment into delight.

About two weeks later, I called the sign company. The official opening of our new facility neared, and I wanted to check that our sign would be installed. When I called, I asked if Ken was there. The man responded he wasn't there. I asked if he knew when Ken might return. He answered, "I'm sorry, he won't be back. Ken died last Friday." I was in shock. Ken was about forty-five years old, seemingly in good health. How hard this blow must have been for his family. But then I rejoiced. I was so thankful God had chosen me to share the gospel with him. How incredible! Through a few moments of humble obedience, Ken will greet me in heaven. How I wish I was more obedient in sharing my faith in other situations. This episode constantly reminds me about the urgency of the gospel.[171]

Reasons for Disobedience

Relational evangelism. There is much discussion today about the role of relationships in evangelism. I am in no way opposed to relational evangelism as long as it's evangelism. We need to purposefully build relationships with those who have yet to trust Christ as their Savior. Quite often in our post-modern culture, a person wants to see what Jesus will do for them, before they are willing to listen to the gospel. If we are living for Christ, building relationships with others will open opportunities to talk with them about Jesus. But I don't believe evangelism actually takes place until the gospel has been verbally shared to the point of decision. Often God uses some type of relationship to support the verbal message, but not always. A downfall of relational evangelism is that a person may never think his friend is ready to hear the gospel. We begin to rely upon ourselves, and our relationships, rather than God. Yes, we need to build relationships with non-Christians, but as author and Pastor Lee Strobel writes, "Friends, it's imperative that we get into a spiritual discussion and eventually point Unchurched Harry or Mary toward Christ as being the only hope for rescue."[172] As God leads, with sensitivity and love, we must creatively pursue sharing the gospel to the point of decision with our neighbors, friends, or acquaintances. Evangelist Billy Graham has said, "The evangelistic harvest is always urgent. The destiny of men (and women) and of nations is always being decided."[173]

Fear of evangelism. We are often afraid of sharing Christ. Paul said, "For I am not ashamed of the gospel, for it is the power of God for salvation to everyone who believes, to the Jew first, and also to the Greek."[174] For some reason, most people in the church today (and admittedly I am sometimes in this group) seem ashamed or afraid to talk about the most important person in history and the most important person in their lives, Jesus Christ. We don't hesitate to show pictures of our kids, or talk about our spouse or fiancée, but we shy away from talking about our Lord. Why is that?

I believe we don't talk to others about Christ because of fear. There are many reasons we're afraid to share the gospel: the fear of being considered fanatics and rejected by our peers; the fear of overestimating a person's readiness that makes us spend more time working at the relationship; the fear of scaring a person off and losing forever the opportunity to talk with them about Christ; the fear of being unable to answer tough questions; the fear of finding God powerless to change lives.

I can write about these fears because I've had them myself. But we must humble ourselves and trust God- His plan, His message, His power. Sometimes we fear because we are afraid of what our listeners will think of us. Yet, the crucified person can forget about self and move forward, sharing the gospel message of Christ's death and resurrection to save sinners. We must humbly forget about our fears, and walk in obedience to His Great Commission.

God does the Work

We also humble ourselves in evangelism when we recognize we can do nothing to change a person's heart. We can have The Four Spiritual Laws memorized, but that will not lead a person to Christ. We can know all the answers to apologetic arguments concerning creation, evil, and the remote native who has never heard the gospel, but unless God touches the heart, the unbeliever's questions only camouflage the disbelief that will always fog the reality of God's love and forgiveness. On the other hand, we might fumble through our testimony or a gospel presentation, but when God's Spirit touches someone's heart, even when people seem not to be listening, they will be ready to receive Christ.

I once called an acquaintance and asked him if I could take him to lunch. I frankly told him that my assignment for our Sunday School class was to share the gospel with someone, and asked if he was interested. He hesitated at first, but then accepted my offer. We had a good time eating, and then I pulled out a copy of The Four Spiritual Laws and we went through it. Danny asked several good questions and we had a nice conversation, but he wasn't ready to receive the gospel. I told him if he ever had any further questions about a personal faith in Christ, I would be happy to talk with him. He took the booklet and we left the restaurant. I was disappointed, but at least we had left on good terms. The next day Danny invited me to a baseball game. We stayed in touch for a while, but I'm not aware that he has ever prayed to receive Christ. At least seeds of the gospel have been sewn into his life.

God calls us to sow seeds.[175] Some will fall on rocks or among thorns, but others will fall on good soil. We can't judge the heart. God is the one who brings regeneration.[176] Therefore we pray the Holy Spirit would go before our path and lead us to people who are ripe. Ken was very ripe. Danny wasn't. But we must be ready to share Christ. If we trust in our own training, our own timing, or in our relationship with the unbeliever, then we are not fully depending on the Holy Spirit and humbling ourselves before Him in obedience. The humble person will use love, sensitivity, and dependence upon the Holy Spirit to be involved in evangelism.

The Next Step

Evangelism is not the last stop in helping fulfill the Great Commission. It's just the first step. The text says, "Go, therefore, and make disciples." The humble disciple will also be involved in discipleship. God wants us to have our cake and eat it too! Just as it's an incredible joy to watch one's own children come into the world, it's a beautiful moment to be involved in leading someone to Christ. But we don't want our children to stay in diapers. There is great fulfillment in watching both our natural and spiritual children develop into mature adults. That was certainly Paul's desire for his spiritual children.[177] He talked of this purpose in Colossians 1:28-29, "And we proclaim Him, admonishing every man and teaching every man with all wisdom, that we may present every man complete in Christ." That is our goal. Not only to win people to Christ, but to build them up in the faith so they may be complete and mature in their relationship with God.

There are many ways a person can help another grow as a disciple of Jesus Christ.[178] You can have your personal Bible study time together. You can attend church and Sunday School together. You can spend time in prayer for them and with them. Your families can go out for pizza together. The key to discipleship is being together.[179] The hard thing for disciple makers is not a lack of training materials, but the time and exhaustive effort that spiritual children require.

I am excited about my children and I love them dearly. But I have had to give up some things because they need me. When my kids were little, my wife couldn't just run to the store and leave them home by themselves. When I arrived home from work, I couldn't just turn on Sports Center and relax in front of the television. There were diapers to change, stories to read, bottles to make, and imaginary playmates to endure. Spiritually young Christians have the same type of needs. Yet for so long we've allowed, even encouraged, believers to remain as infants and toddlers. No one has taken the time to train them because it wasn't a priority.

Training disciples is an arduous task. Paul wrote in Colossians 1:29, "And for this purpose also I labor, striving[180] according to His power, which mightily works within me."

We must humbly ask God to give us the time, energy, and wisdom to nurture those spiritual babes whom we have helped bring into the world. Further, we must ask God to help us care for spiritual babes who have been left at our door steps. Many in the church today have come to Christ at an early age, but have never been trained. They are still in diapers. We must help them grow in Christ through investing our lives in them.

When my son started eating solid food, we gave him Zwieback crackers. A Zwieback is more like a piece of bark than a cracker, and it makes an incredible mess as the child salivates all over it. But it did help him learn how to chew, and it was good for his gums and the teething process. I've never taken the opportunity to try a Zwieback myself, but I can't imagine having trouble eating one. I have a full set of teeth, and have tackled hard crunchy foods. However, my son only had two teeth, and there were a few times the cracker caught in his throat and he started to choke. Kathy and I couldn't even leave the room. We had to put his needs before our own.

We must put others' needs before our own when mentoring others. We must schedule time to minister to spiritual children. A Sunday school teacher should not just show up to class and forget about her students the rest of the week. An adult fellowship group leader should not just teach on Wednesday nights. The leader should invest his life into those who want to grow in Christ. Prayerfully, in a few months, spiritual children will have learned how to feed themselves correctly with the Word. They will have learned how to communicate with God through prayer. They will share the gospel with others. And some day, they will have their own spiritual children and we will become spiritual grandparents.

There are many people in the church today running around in diapers because no one is helping them grow. Many churches have in-fighting, and even split, because members are not mature in Christ. As spiritual children mature, there will be less sibling rivalry. They will grow in their sensitivity and love toward fellow Christians. And as we mature, we'll have a more effective witness in our culture.

Humble disciples must be committed to Christ's mandate. As Navigator's founder Dawson Trotman was so apt to say, "Where is your man?" Who are the people you are investing your life in so they might make disciples?

To All the Nations

There is a third aspect of the Great Commission. Jesus not only said, "Go" and "Make disciples." He said "Go, therefore, and make disciples of all the nations." From the beginning of the ages, God has been concerned about nations knowing Him. He often used Israel as a testimony to the nations of the world.[181] Isaiah 45:22 says, "Turn to Me, and be saved, all the ends of the earth; For I am God, and there is no other."

In the New Testament we have the mandate to preach to all the nations.[182] Acts 1:8 reminds us to be witnesses even to the remotest parts of the earth.

Throughout history, God has used events to help proclaim the gospel to all peoples. He used the persecution of the early church to spread the gospel throughout the Middle East, Europe, and beyond.[183] Explorers from Spain and Portugal were joined by missionaries who took the gospel into far off lands. The printing press made the gospel possible to many peoples of the world. God caused the persecution of Christians in Europe to bring pilgrims to a new land and lay a foundation of righteousness that would be a beacon to the world.

We in the United States should allow God to use us in preaching the gospel to all nations. He did it before through a humble haystack prayer meeting of college students.[184] He did it before through a humble shoe clerk who wanted to give his life wholly to God.[185] He did it before through a humble student distributing Spanish Bibles.[186] He wants to use us continually, but we must make ourselves available to Him. We must give our lives to be clean vessels filled with His Spirit and His compassion for the world.

Two-thirds of the world's population, more than 3.2 billion people, live in the 10/40 window where ninety-five percent of the people are unevangelized, many never having heard the gospel. There are 2550 unreached tribal groups with a total population of 140 million people.[187] We, who have been blessed with so much, must give up our rights and readily share the abundance God has given us with the world. We must humble ourselves and follow God's heart for the world.

Our attitude can become like the chauffeur who drove a wealthy couple from the East to California. First they became lost in the Nevada desert, then their car broke down. The situation became desperate. The chauffeur toiled under the car's hood every day, but could not get the engine started. The fierce heat took its toll until finally both the wealthy man and his wife weakened and died. When a search party finally reached the scene, they found the chauffeur still alive. Why? Because every day, under the car's hood, he drank water from the radiator, but shared none with his employers.[188]

The chauffeur was not wrong to drink the water himself, but he was wrong not to share the water with others. God has given us great resources concerning the living water, but we must share these resources with the rest of the world.[189]

Many Resources to Share

We must share our prayers with the world. We can use prayer guides such as Operation World[190] and the prayer letters of missionaries we personally support to pray strategically. We can use denominational prayer lists or we can gain information from our local church missions committee. It is critical we pray for those on the front lines of the spiritual battle.

We are to share our riches with the world. America is the richest country in the world, and yet we are also very materialistic. We need to give cheerfully and sacrificially to those who are starving physically, but even more so to those who are starving spiritually. Each of us has the opportunity through personal giving and our church's missions budget to give to global missionary work that honors Christ. It may mean buying a used car rather than a new one to help purchase a computer for a new church in Brussels. It may mean going out to eat one less time each month to support a youth worker in Kenya. We must put others' needs before our own luxuries and consider how God might use our riches for His glory.

The abundance of trained professionals in our American churches must be shared with the world. In many countries, there is an appalling lack of trained disciple makers and pastors. Therefore, we should send teachers into seminaries and Bible colleges overseas to help train these people. We can send church planters into countries and train nationals to be disciple makers. Groups such as R.I.M.I. and Gospel for Asia are training and sending nationals as church planters and pastors quite effectively. We can also help support nationals who are studying in the United States with our financial and prayer support, plus through developing personal friendships with them.

Further, we must share our lives with the world. This may be hosting a missionary who is home on furlough or sending an encouraging e-mail to one far away. As God leads, this may mean going ourselves on a short-term (or longer) missionary experience. It's amazing what God can do in and through your life when you minister in another culture, but you must give Him the time. I believe it would be great if every Christian spent some significant time in a missions environment. It might be a summer helping an inner-city church or three months helping to plant a church in Moscow. And, as the Spirit leads, there will be some who are called by God to spend more than a couple of months in another culture or country. As part of my internship at seminary, my wife and I spent five months working at a church in Clacton-on-Sea, England. I have also spent two weeks doing evangelism and discipleship in Craiova, Romania, and two weeks doing evangelism and servant ministries in Russia. All of these have been life-changing experiences.

God has provided the water through the well-spring Jesus Christ. He has commanded us to go to all nations and distribute the living water of the gospel. If you will spend a day, a week, a month, or even longer in a different culture, your life will take on new perspective. The Great Commission will become more real. You will begin to understand God's heart for the world.

What is God's purpose for the humble Christian? He has commissioned us to make disciples of all nations. We should ask ourselves: "Am I helping fulfill God's purpose for the Church?" "Am I sharing my faith in Christ with others?" "Am I investing my life in others as a disciple maker?" "Am I giving my life to reach the world with gospel?" Only by sticking to God's business plan, will the Church truly be successful. Let us deny ourselves, and humbly commit ourselves to being involved in the Great Commission for the glory of God.

A Suggested Prayer:

Lord, I confess I've not been involved in the Great Commission as much as I should. I ask You to give me Your compassion for those who don't know You. Help me look for and pursue opportunities to lovingly share Your gospel. Help me formally and informally invest in those around me who already know You. And make me more of a world Christian, Father. Thank You Jesus that You died for each person, from every tribe, around the globe. Make me ever mindful to share my resources and energy to benefit all people that they might know Your love and grace. In Jesus' name, Amen.

Chapter 10

The Service of Humility

Columnist Cal Thomas found himself called "a Christian leader." He wondered what it meant. Did it mean more speaking engagements? Would he be asked to appear on Christian talk shows? Thomas says, "It would certainly give me the right to start putting Scripture references under my signed name in books I have written. I would surely sign more Bibles, which I find a curious practice since I didn't write that Book." Cal Thomas went on to give a picture of whom he would call a Christian leader.

> In a church I once attended, there was a man of tremendous faith. His wife was an alcoholic. His daughter had psychological problems. He was often poor in health. Yet, week after week, he never complained. He always smiled and asked me how I was doing. He faithfully brought to church a young blind man who had no transportation. He always sat with the blind man, helping him sing the hymns by saying the words into his ear.

> That man was a 'Christian leader' if ever there was one.[191]

We could also say that man was a Christian servant.

The obedient disciple will be a humble servant. Jesus set an example of service often. Possibly the most outstanding passage we have concerning the servant-heart of Jesus is in Mark 10:45, "For even the Son of Man did not come to be served, but to serve, and to give His life a ransom for many." Jesus didn't come to earth to strut His power and position. He came to minister to our greatest need—reconciliation with the Father. We are to follow in Christ's footsteps, get our minds off ourselves, and give our lives for the sake of others.

Some have the title of servant but are not really servants at all. A nurse can change bed pans and give shots to the weak, but unless she is joyously giving herself to others, she is not truly a servant. She may grudgingly go through the motions, not touching hearts but just picking up a paycheck. Elected officials are sometimes called public servants. Yet for many years, the public has felt abused, not served, by many in government.

However, the Christian walking in the power of the Holy Spirit should be a servant. This is not through obtaining a title, but through acquiring an attitude. The famous orchestra conductor Leonard Bernstein was once asked to name the most difficult instrument to play. He responded quickly, "Second fiddle. I can get plenty of first violinists, but to find one who plays second violin with as much enthusiasm or second French horn or second flute, now that's a problem. And yet if no one plays second, we have no harmony."[192] We need men and women, leaders and followers, who will give their hearts and lives in service. Doing this, no matter what the cost, is a fragrant offering to God and others. The humble disciple will forget about self and will serve. Let us look at several characteristics of the humble servant.

A Good Example

No matter who we are or what we are doing, people are always watching us. I remember when my family began to know our neighbors after moving to our new home. One of my neighbors asked me if I was a minister. I told him I was. Then I asked, "What was it about my life that made you think I was a minister?" He said he'd seen me reading a lot on my back deck, and he knew that ministers read a lot. Isn't it amazing what people perceive? What are people perceiving about you? Could they guess you're a Christian because of your kind and gentle nature? Could they guess you follow Christ because of your servant's heart?

One of the ways we can be an example for others is by only asking people to do what we have done ourselves. People around us need to know we are servants. It's important for leaders occasionally to do tasks not usually associated with a leader's job description (like cleaning out a restroom or helping move furniture). Obviously this wouldn't always be the best use of their time or gifts. It may even stop others from using their gifts in the body of Christ or deprive others of needed income. But doing menial tasks reminds us we are to serve as leaders. We are no better, or worse, than anyone else. We are just different in the kingdom of God.

Take a moment to think on Ruth Harms Calkin's poem I Wonder.

You know, Lord, how I serve You with great
emotional fervor in the limelight.
You know how eagerly I speak for You at a women's club.
You know my genuine enthusiasm at a Bible study.
But how would I react, I wonder,
if You pointed to a basin of water
and asked me to wash the callused feet

> of a bent and wrinkled old woman
> day after day, month after month, in a room
> where nobody saw and nobody knew?[193]

How would I respond? How would you?

He Washed their Feet

Jesus knew about washing others' feet. What an incredible act of service and humility the ultimate leader displayed as He girded the towel and took up the basin. This happened on the night of His betrayal, the eve of His crucifixion. Christ would have been justified to tell the men to leave their feet dirty, for this was a custom of mourning. And yet, on their last evening together, His greatest act of service was not to leave His best-seller for His group to distribute, or to dole a bountiful financial sum to each person for the time they'd given to Him. His gift to them was to wash their feet. He gave them an example of servitude and humility that would change their lives, the church, and the world.

During this time in Middle East history, most people wore open sandals. Walking down dirt roads made one's feet filthy. Usually when a person entered a home, the host provided a basin of water to allow the guest to wash his feet. Sometimes a hired servant would do this task—the most lowly deed the servant could do.[194]

At the Last Supper, the disciples had a dispute.[195] They argued among themselves about who was the greatest. At this decisive moment, Jesus girded the towel and washed their feet.[196] What a powerful picture. They must have gulped hard as they recognized their own hubris in light of their Master's humility. Then Jesus said to them,

> Do you know what I have done to you? You call
> Me Teacher and Lord; and you are right, for so I

> am. If I then, the Lord and the Teacher, washed your feet, you also ought to wash one another's feet. For I gave you an example that you also should do as I did to you (John 13:12-15).

We should gulp hard today. We often seek greatness through power, position, money, status, promotions, recognition, good looks, and fame. Jesus said we need to stoop down and serve as slaves for one another. In God's eyes and in God's kingdom, the greatest among us shall be the servant.[197] The greatest among us shall be the one who visits orphans and widows,[198] the one who helps the blind man sing a hymn. On God's scale, the greatest among us is the one who anonymously and sacrificially gives the widow's mite. He or she is the one who will hear, "Well, done, good and faithful slave."[199] When we are asked to help clean up after an office party, do we look for an excuse to leave, or gladly serve to the glory of God? If someone needs a ride to a church function, do we gladly volunteer when it's possible, or do we always see others' needs as an inconvenience to us? The humble disciple will do what he or she can to serve others.

Give Your Best

Demanding excellence is not always necessary. I shouldn't expect an immaculate house when I come home from work, for my wife has been spending much time home schooling our three children. Excellence in housekeeping is not a priority for her at this time. It's not necessary for me to spend an excruciating amount of time drawing the most precise picture I can when I am coloring with my children. My intensity level doesn't need to be extreme if I'm playing a pick up basketball game in the driveway.

But when working or encouraging others, we should do things with excellence to the glory of God. This doesn't mean we'll be perfect, but we want to do the best job we can with the resources we have. Whether you're planting flowers at the church, crafting a gift, writing a contract which will give you a big bonus, or reading to your child, the true servant seeks to serve God with excellence as an act of love and gratitude. "And whatever you do in word or deed, do all in the name of the Lord Jesus, giving thanks through Him to God the Father" (Colossians 3:17). Our desire to do the best job we can with the resources we have tells God "thank You."

With this attitude, our audience of One is always the same, and we avoid the trap of only being a people-pleaser. We avoid doing our best only when others are around. Are you consistently diligent at work whether your boss is present or absent? Let us be reminded that our God is omnipresent and He enjoys His children doing their best. Whether at work or home, whether getting paid or volunteering, it's the Lord whom we serve.[200] We should want, as His slaves, to give Him glory in all we do.[201]

The summer after receiving my Master of Divinity degree, Kathy and I both needed summer jobs. Each of us had one more year of schooling which began in the fall. She found work at a large toy store. I became the most well-educated hamburger flipper at a fast-food restaurant. I was promoted to working the drive-through window before I left. An interesting phenomenon happened several times during that summer. I always laughed when another restaurant in the chain informed us that a district manager was on the way to inspect our restaurant. As soon as our manager hung up the phone, everyone scurried to make sure our place was in order. Floors were swept, the salad bar was freshened, and French fry containers were restocked. We certainly wanted to please the district manager. But if the goal of the restaurant was to serve customers, then we should always have been on our best behavior.

As Christians, we should remember our Owner is always watching. He holds us accountable. Let us glorify Him by giving our best.

"I Need You"

Servants are often portrayed as martyrs who don't ask for help, but do everything themselves. A martyr is the independent gunslinger who fights off the band of ornery rustlers in John Wayne style. She is the Sunday school superintendent who takes three hours to call all the children on a Saturday evening. She feels like it's her duty, and she doesn't want to bother the Sunday school teachers, so she just does it herself. A martyr is the pastor who rarely takes a day off because the church depends so heavily upon him. There's so much to do and certainly his family will understand the sacrifice they must make for God's work.

We're thankful for hard workers who are committed to their responsibilities. But we must be careful not to imagine we're the only ones whom God should or can use. People who believe they are too important to take a day off have their life out of balance and are proud and selfish. The best pianist in the church should occasionally take a week off. The pastor should ask others to help with visitation.

It's hard for many of us to ask for and accept help from others, yet we should readily admit we can't do everything ourselves. Let us enjoy the fellowship and encouragement others bring into our lives. When we walk in the power of the Holy Spirit, focusing on others, we gain joy from helping others. The Apostle Paul reminded us of Jesus' words, "that He Himself said, 'It is more blessed to give than to receive.'"[202] Let us, therefore, be willing to ask others for help on occasion. Maybe we need child care, a ride to church, or help fixing our car. We must be careful not to think we are so valuable or gifted that we don't need, or shouldn't ask for, help from others.

We should assume that if others can't help at the time they will honestly tell us. If they don't want to help us with a specific task, they will lovingly say so. Let us assume they are mature in Christ until they prove us wrong. It's okay to ask for help when we really want or need it. This can make someone else feel needed and valuable. Even when we could do the job ourselves, it may be good to ask another for help. It can be a wonderful time of fellowship and a great time of training. There will come a time when you should no longer be the person to lead the fellowship group or set up the chairs in the sanctuary. You must delegate and allow others to grow and use their gifts in the body of Christ.

Here is a bold, but obvious example. Many senior pastors can teach Sunday school as well as most people in their congregation, if not better. Most pastors have a teaching gift and specific training in how to teach. Should all pastors, therefore, teach all of the adult and children's classes? Plainly not! The pastor can't be twelve places at once. He may not have a passion to teach Sunday school or the time to do it. Allowing others to develop their gifts of teaching and leading is crucial. By doing this, they will know the joy of ministering and using their gifts to the glory of God. God will use the service of each individual uniquely in expressing His love and grace. And I'm sure we'll find many lay people who can teach better than their pastor if given the chance! This example can be broadened to so many different settings. We must learn to delegate and not hoard responsibility ourselves.

As you seek the assistance of others, allow them to use their creativity. Give them the space they need to make decisions and even mistakes. They won't do everything as you do. At times, you may need to offer suggestions or correct a careless person in love. It's humbling to refrain from correcting someone when they are doing something differently. Sometimes it's better to allow others to learn from their mistakes than for you to correct them repeatedly. We learn as we try, not exclusively by watching someone else. Believe their heart is in the right place until they prove you wrong. Assume they are seeking to serve with excellence. Remember, you don't do everything perfectly either. When others seek to serve the Lord with excellence, don't be too critical. Accountability is essential, but we should not be overly critical.

The legend is told of a desert wanderer who found a crystal spring of unsurpassed freshness. The water was so pure the wanderer decided to take some to his king. Barely satisfying his own thirst, he filled a leather bottle with the clear liquid and carried it many days beneath the desert sun before he reached the palace. When he finally laid his offering at the feet of his sovereign, the water had become stale and rank due to the old container in which it had been stored. But the king wouldn't let his faithful subject even imagine it was unfit for use. He tasted it with expressions of gratitude and delight, and sent away the loyal heart filled with gladness. After he had gone, others sampled it and expressed their surprise that the king had even pretended to enjoy it. "Ah!" said he, "it was not the water I tasted, but the love that prompted the offering."[203]

Many times our service is marked by multiplied imperfections, but the Master looks at our motives and says "It's good." God is not overly critical of our imperfect offerings of service to Him. Let us not be too quick to criticize those who are serving to the glory of God.

Handling Praise

Leaders are continually tempted by pride. If we try to please God with our best efforts, people will notice our good work and often give us accolades. We may receive a certificate for a job well done, or a plaque signifying years of service. People may appreciate our talents and applaud. How should the humble respond?

It's tough to accept compliments without being pious or braggadocios. Yet, to deny others' compliments is to disregard God's work in and through us. We should trust the comments are sincere, and that our deed has been encouraging. We can respond with a simple "thank you" or "I am glad God used that in your life." To say "You really don't mean it" or "It was nothing" is not truly acknowledging God working through you. Saying "Thank you, your comment is an encouragement to me" tells well-wishers that their words are of value to you. Then you can move on to another topic without drawing great attention to yourself.[204] In every setting we want to point praise to God.

Let the servant also be generous and truthful in his or her praise toward others. Insecure leaders don't praise others. They're afraid to admit others have done a good job, sometimes even better than they could do. But praise and encouragement is very important in the body of Christ and in the world. It prompts others to use their gifts in the church. Commending others helps us remember we're not the only ones who can glorify and serve God. A short phone call can go a long way to pick up the morale of a faithful club leader. A "thank you" note to an assistant or secretary at work can bring out the best in a person. Moreover, through encouragement you show the love of Christ. As servants, we must forget about ourselves. We must continue to ask how we can glorify God and better serve others.

At an awards reception, one of a group of reporters asked Corrie ten Boom, "Don't you have trouble keeping humble after being honored so greatly?" Without hesitation, she answered, "When Christ was riding into Jerusalem and people were throwing palm branches in His way, crying all honor to Him, do you think the donkey thought it was for him? I am but a donkey and know these honors are for Christ alone."[205]

Let us be humble donkeys, servants, who give all glory and praise to God.

A Suggested Prayer:

What a privilege, O Lord, to serve You! I seek to praise and honor You with all You've given me. Help me honor You with diligence, creativity, and a heart of service. If I should gain any accolades from the world, help me always walk in humility, remembering Who allowed me to achieve any measure of success. Let me always remember, ultimately, You are my Audience. I seek to please You, My Master. In Jesus' name, Amen.

Chapter 11

The Esteem of Humility

"I am so stupid!" "I can't do anything right!" "Nobody really cares about me." These are thoughts some of us have said out loud, and all occasionally have wallowing in their minds. Where do these thoughts come from? Why do we bash ourselves with thoughts leading to frustration and discouragement? These ideas of self-flagellation come from comparing ourselves to the unrealistic standards in our world.

Some of these thoughts come from the media. We are not as wealthy as Malcom Forbes, Jr. We are not as glamorous as super model Kathy Ireland. We don't have the power and prestige of the wrestler, "The Rock." Even though most don't admit it, these extremes create standards for our lives we try to emulate. Realizing we'll never have the fame, fortune, or power of James Bond, we begin to feel of little value. "If I could only win the lottery," we may dream, "then I would really be a somebody."

Some of us heard false declarations from our parents or other adults when we were growing up. A single "You're so stupid!" or "You'll never amount to anything" can devastate children whose esteem often rests in the hands of the adults around them.

We also get false ideas from comparing ourselves to people around us. Our neighbor has a nicer car. The friend we graduated with has a higher salary. Our sister has a better singing voice. We accumulate people around us who seem to be better in everything. The aggregate effect of our false thinking is mediocrity. We believe we can't do anything well, so we quit trying. We settle into a mediocre maintenance mentality. Our only purpose in life becomes existence.

There is another enemy who gives us a wrong perspective. He is our arch rival, the devil. He seeks to devour and defeat us any way he can.[206] The devil often reminds us of past sin to make us feel undue remorse and guilt. Satan may do this to the point where we try to pay for our sins by good works. He wants believers to feel useless in the body of Christ. As we struggle with sin, Satan tells us the lie we'll never gain victory, but will constantly be frustrated and defeated.

As we listen to the world and our enemy, our self-image steadily lowers. We see other's perfection, and the multitude of our own imperfections. We feel insignificant as only a minute particle on a giant globe. We think, "God can't use me. I'm a nobody."

Please know this: humility is not saying you're a nobody! To say or believe you are a nobody is a lie. You are a somebody. You are extremely precious and significant in the eyes of God. It doesn't matter how you compare to the world or how it perceives you. It's God's view that counts. As believers, we should have a proper perspective of ourselves in Jesus Christ. We may not have fancy clothes, but we wear a robe of righteousness. We may not have bundles of cash, but we have an incredible inheritance. We must gain the right perspective of ourselves in Christ.

Paul wrote in Romans 12:3, "For through the grace given to me I say to every man among you not to think more highly of himself than he ought to think; but to think so as to have sound judgment, as God has allotted to each a measure of faith." Certainly we should not boast of our own merits. That would be thinking "too highly." God is the one who endowed us with certain talents.

But Paul didn't say we are to think of ourselves as the scum of the earth, either. No, we are to think of ourselves with sound judgment.[207] We can boast in the things God has done in and through us.[208] The best way to balance our thinking is to consider what God said about us in Jesus Christ.

Given His Image

> Then God said, "Let Us make man in Our image, according to Our likeness; and let them rule over the fish of the sea and over the birds of the sky and over the cattle and over all the earth, and over every creeping thing that creeps on the earth." And God created man in His own image, in the image of God He created him; male and female He created them (Genesis 1:26-27).

What does being created in the image of God mean? Award-winning author Dr. Paul Brand writes, "God's image is not an arrangement of skin cells or a physical shape, but rather an inbreathed spirit."[209] God formed man from the dust, and then gave man life through breathing spirit into him. Through this God-given spirit we attain attributes that are in the likeness of God, such as personality, creativity, and reason. Of "image," Old Testament scholar Allen Ross says,

> It doesn't signify a physical representation of corporeality, for God is a spirit. The term must therefore figuratively describe human life as a

> reflection of God's spiritual nature; that is, human life has the communicated attributes that came with the inbreathing (Genesis 2:7).[210]

How special we are! No other part of God's creation was given life through God breathing spirit into their flesh. Apologist Josh McDowell states, "God has given you and me something He never gave any other part of His creation—His image. We have the ability to think, to will, to love, to create, to make moral decisions."[211] Daily, we should remind ourselves how special we are to God. Out of all His creation, humans alone have the breath of the Almighty breathed into them. And when He was done creating Adam He said Man was very good.[212]

We are Unique

Our uniqueness in the body of Christ is another reason we can think highly of ourselves. In Romans 12:4, Paul uses the analogy of the physical body. He says, "For just as we have many members in one body and all the members don't have the same function, so we, who are many, are one body in Christ, and individually members one of another." Each member of our physical body has different functions, some being more essential for the body. Even so, each part must be in perfect use for the body to function at its highest and most efficient level.

A thumbnail is often taken for granted, yet if we smash it with a hammer, our whole body writhes with pain. For many days, until the nail is healed, the nail is sensitive. We have to be careful how we hold a pen or open a door. Our lives are changed. We must now pay attention to our measly thumbnail. To eliminate or cripple any part of our frame makes us less than what God intended us to be and hinders our existence, even if only in small ways.

Each of us is crucial in the body of Christ. All have at least one gift to contribute. The humble person will work hard to develop the gifts God has given, and always remember God is the gift-giver. Hard work and training only enhance the gifts God has given. The Apostle Paul wrote, "But to each one of us grace was given according to the measure of Christ's gift" (Ephesians 4:7). Once we recognize these gifts, we are to use them for the building up of one another in the body of Christ (Ephesians 4:12, 13).

We have many immature Christians in the church today because few people in the body of Christ have been using their gifts. Some have been proudly denying they have any gifts. This is false humility. Again, Paul wrote in Ephesians 4 that each one has been gifted by God. Some acknowledge their gifts, but then refuse to use them. As a result, the church is hindered and part of the body withers into uselessness.

It's selfish to keep our gifts to ourselves. It's selfish to deny that God has gifted us for His glory. When we don't use our gifts, others must compensate. They have to fill in for us and are distracted from focusing on their God-given abilities.

Using the Wrong Tools

It takes more energy to do work when we lack the best tools. I remember trying to put together a home entertainment center with a screw driver. I got the job done after about four hours of perseverance. If I had an electric screwdriver, which I now own, the task would have taken me about an hour.

Some people are not especially gifted in working with children, but they do it sacrificially because no one else seems to be available. This saps their strength and eventually takes away joy in ministry. Ministerial burn-out, trying to be all things to all people, is a sad reality both for pastors and laity alike. It's a travesty, in financial giving and especially in service, that the 80/20 rule usually holds true. Eighty percent of the people do 20 percent of the work in a local church, and 20 percent of the people do 80 percent of the work. This is not the formula for good health and growth. This is the formula for a heart attack. To be a healthy, mature body, every member must do its part. **No one can do the job God has given to you as effectively as you can!** Every member must be a minister. Every church should want to live by the 100/100 rule.

I have always been a reluctant leader. Throughout my life, I've been thrust into leadership positions and given opportunities to speak. Yet, I didn't feel I had the gifts to do either. Even when people told me I encouraged them, I didn't want to admit God may have gifted me to preach. Finally, after three years of seminary, I decided maybe God had given me so much training and many speaking opportunities because He had gifted me to preach His Word.

In my last year of seminary, I purposely worked at developing my speaking skills. I applied for and received a teaching fellowship in the homiletics department. As a teaching fellow, I reviewed many sermons of young seminarians just beginning their formal training. This was very helpful for my own development. I also took more preaching classes and had the opportunity to rub shoulders with gifted homileticians on the staff. This was a wonderful year of training and preparation for me. There are certainly areas in my life where He has not gifted me, such as working with my hands. But I wouldn't be fulfilling my role in the body of Christ if I didn't develop and use the gifts of preaching and teaching He has given me.

Fulfilling our Roles

The family is suffering in our society today. Many families are breaking down because the roles of men and women are being confused and undermined by jealousy, envy, and a false need for power and wealth. Men have become unwilling to take the lead in their homes, so women assume the responsibility. Some wives may refuse to submit to their husbands, so they become defensive and quit trying to lovingly lead their wives. Children observe this struggle and begin to feel guilt which they are unable to handle. Thus, a multitude of families become inactive or broken due to each member not functioning as God has planned.[213]

It's the same in the body of Christ. When we are unwilling to submit to our God-given roles, the church is dysfunctional. When we neglect our God-given gifts for the building up of Christ's church and the proclaiming the gospel, the church is impaired.

What are your gifts?[214] Are you a seamstress? Are you a teacher? Do you enjoy cooking and inviting people into your home? Maybe God has granted you the ability to speak or to pray with a fervent heart. Do you work well with numbers or with your hands? Maybe you enjoy financial blessings and have the gift of giving. Ask your pastor or church leaders where you might be used to the glory of God. All are to be equipped and encouraged by the leadership of the church, "for the work of service, to the building up of the body of Christ; until we all attain to the unity of the faith, and of the knowledge of the Son of God, to a mature man, to the measure of the stature which belongs to the fullness of Christ."[215]

Whatever your gift is, you are unique and special in the body of Christ. God only made one of you! Now He wants each of us to minister to one another and the world by using our God-given talents and gifts for His glory.

Our Great Value

One final reason we can think highly (not too highly) of

ourselves in Christ: He died for us. God counted each of us worthy of His Son's death.

If you studied economics, you would find the real value of any item is the cost someone is willing to pay for it. If you went into a golf store, you might pay $500 to $1000 for a full set of clubs. At a discount store you could get a set of clubs for less. Yet, sometimes clubs sell for more. When John F. Kennedy's clubs were auctioned by Sotheby's, it was estimated they would sell for between $700 and $900. Yet his set of woods sold for $772,500 and the irons went for $387,500.[216] The more we value something, the more we are willing to pay for it.

If this is truly the means of determining value, we must realize God considers us extremely valuable and precious. He paid the highest price, His only Son, to redeem us from the penalty of our sins. "For God so loved the world, that He gave His only begotten Son, that whoever believes in Him should not perish, but have eternal life" (John 3:16). He "so loves" each of us. Paul wrote, "But God demonstrates His own love toward us, in that while we were yet sinners, Christ died for us" (Romans 5:8). God knew we were a sinful, rebellious people. Yet in spite of our unfaithfulness, He considered us worthy of His Son's death. We were bought with a great price.[217]

We couldn't pay for our own salvation. We did nothing to deserve Jesus, but God freely brought us into a right relationship with God as His gift to us.[218] All we have to do is accept the gift! The wrath of God against us was halted by the blood of His Son.[219]

Never say you're a nobody. You're a somebody! God gave the greatest price, His only unique Son, so you might have eternal life.

How do you think of yourself? Do you say, "I'm not special"; "God can't use me"; "Nobody cares for me"? That's not humility. That's being full of pride and calling

God a liar! We must view ourselves with humility, but we can also think highly of ourselves because we are in Christ. God gave us His image. God gave us His gifts. God gave us His Son. Don't say you're a nobody. You are a special, significant Somebody in the eyes of God.

A Suggested Prayer:

Thank You, Lord, that I'm a Somebody because of all You've done for me. Thank You so much that You created me with Your image and gave me gifts to be used for Your glory. And thank You most of all that You counted me as so special that You sent Jesus, Your only Son, to die on the cross for me. Help me to no longer think of myself in wrong, sinful ways, but help me to use the gifts and blessings You've given me to exalt Your Holy Name. In Jesus' name, Amen.

Chapter 12

The Stewardship of Humility

A wealthy Christian lady walked by a ragged looking man standing on the street corner. Their eyes met and her soft heart melted. Being a generous soul, she walked over to him and gave him a five-dollar bill.

"Here's some money for you," she said with a smile, "God's speed." She thought nothing of it. She often helped the unfortunate. The next day, as the Christian walked the same route, again she saw the shabbily dressed man. Thinking it imprudent to give another handout, she attempted to elude the vagabond. This time however, the man came to her, pressing a bill in her hand.

"Here's your hundred dollars," he said. "God's Speed came in first and paid twenty to one."[220]

There is much confusion about money today. Most of us in the United States have sufficient financial resources to provide food and shelter for our families. Even those who aren't as fortunate can often find help through social programs and churches.[221] Still, many of us don't feel rich. With a home mortgage, car payments, and credit card debt, we often owe more than we own.

Advertisers prey on our materialistic inclinations. Sponsors dished out approximately $70,000 per second for a commercial during the Super Bowl in 2003 because they know the lusts of the eyes are very powerful.

What we used to call greed, we now call need. How much is enough? As believers in Jesus Christ, we see all kinds of needs around us. How much should we give to the church, to ministries, and to other organizations? How much should we keep for ourselves and our families? What does the Bible have to say about finances? In the midst of great wealth and many demands, how can the disciple of Christ submit to God in the stewardship of money?

How much is Enough?

Jesus gave us sound teaching about wealth in Luke 12. After discussing with His disciples the importance of trusting God during persecution, someone in the surrounding throng changed the subject.

> And someone in the crowd said to Him, "Teacher, tell my brother to divide the family inheritance with me." But He said to him, "Man, who appointed Me a judge or arbiter over you?" And He said to them, "Beware, and be on your guard against every form of greed; for not even when one has an abundance does his life consist of his possessions" (Luke 12:13-15).[222]

The first financial principle Jesus shared is: we should not hoard wealth. Jesus knew the greed of both brothers. One lusted after his inheritance, and the other wouldn't allow the inheritance to be distributed. They were both greedy.[223]

We are not to be greedy. We should set some type of limit to our needs. Our materialistic age has the slogan, "He who dies with the most toys wins."[224] Greed brings neither peace nor contentment. Greed only brings constant frustration because one is never satisfied. Enough is never enough. John D. Rockefeller was once asked how much money it would take to be really satisfied. He answered, "Just a little bit more!"[225]

Once people accumulate wealth and feel they can relax and enjoy it, they find that life doesn't consist in their possessions. The true value and meaning behind our possessions and wealth are the relationships we have gained or lost in accumulating our assets. The foundational relationship for true contentment is a relationship with God through Christ. One of the wealthiest men who ever lived, King Solomon, said, "He who loves money will not be satisfied with money, nor he who loves abundance with its income. This too is vanity (Ecclesiastes 5:10)."

This is why many people struggle with retirement. They thought they'd be satisfied without work and living off their pensions, retirement accounts and Social Security checks. But it isn't so. Whatever our income, fulfillment doesn't come through our money. Fulfillment comes through the relationships we have at work, at home, and with God that bring true meaning to our lives. Free time without meaningful relationships quickly becomes meaningless.

Paul wrote from his prison cell in Rome, "I have learned to be content in whatever circumstances I am."[226] Paul's secret to contentment was his relationship with Jesus Christ. Of contentment, he says, "I can do all things through Him who strengthens me."[227] Paul also gained great encouragement, no matter what his circumstances, from the brothers and sisters who had helped him throughout his ministry.[228] Contentment comes through our relationships, not through hoarding wealth and possessions. We can never have enough sound relationships of trust and encouragement. But all of us need to come to a point in our lives where we can say, "I have enough," material possessions.

Are you at a point in your life where you can say, "I have enough. If I never got another pay raise, a larger home, or a nicer car, I have enough?" And if you can't say that now, what is your standard? Prayerfully ask God what your financial requirements should be. Have an idea of what size house you really need. Set goals to save for a car, retirement, and your children's education. All of us will have different financial needs and goals, but once we achieve an adequate income, with ample accommodations and accouterments, let us not just keep buying bigger and/or better. That's greed. Some of us may need to down-size. If so, we should confess our materialism and hoarding to God.

What can You Afford?

Most families dream of owning their own home. Kathy and I had lived in four different apartments before we prayerfully began to consider purchasing a home. We felt God wanted us to stay in Lee's Summit, Missouri for many years, and our church now had a solid financial base.

As we began looking at houses, we surmised we could afford payments of approximately nine hundred dollars. Therefore, we looked for homes in the $95,000 range. However, as we viewed many homes over several weeks, we never felt a sense of peace. Did God want us to commit that much money each month to a home, even though we could afford it? We decided to drop our price range by $10,000. Almost immediately, God led us to a home that excited us.

What we can afford is not always what we should purchase. Our money should not be tied to interest and loans when possible. The extra fifty dollars each month Kathy and I had could go toward ministry needs, further paying off our loan, or simply putting food on our table. We could have bought a nicer home, but I'm thankful we didn't.

Jesus told this parable of greed:

> The land of a certain rich man was very productive. And he began reasoning to himself, saying, "What shall I do, since I have no place to store my crops?" And he said, "This is what I will do: I will tear down my barns and build larger ones, and there I will store all my grain and my goods" (Luke 12:16-18).

Here was a man who had an over-abundance. His barns were full of crops. His business was successful. So he decided to keep the excess for himself.

The rich man went on to say, "And I will say to my soul, 'Soul, you have many goods laid up for many years to come; take your ease, eat, drink and be merry.'" But God said to him, "You fool! This very night your soul is required of you; and now who will own what you have prepared?" (Luke 12:19-20).

Saving for Retirement

In what are you investing? For what are you saving? Are you hoarding wealth in a life insurance policy or a stock portfolio so you can retire in leisure? Is your purpose in life to eat, drink, and be merry, especially in your latter years?

We should realistically plan for our golden years. The Social Security system was never meant to be a full retirement plan for anyone, only a supplement. Some believe the baby boomers will bankrupt the system in a few years. It's appropriate to prayerfully develop a savings plan, through pension plans, retirement accounts, stocks, bonds, and other vehicles.

But how much is enough? And does God really want us to completely retire? Certainly, our bodies will slow. For some of us, our current occupation will be an impossibility past our sixty-fifth year. But we should never selfishly waste our lives and stop using our God-given gifts. For many of us, our jobs or hobbies could help support us in later years.

Think of it. Abraham, Moses, and others didn't find their niche until way past retirement age.[229] Financial consultant Larry Burkett says, "I am convinced that retirement, as our generation knows it, is not scriptural.... The concept of idling the majority of people at such an early age is a modern innovation, not a biblical principle."[230] God has so much more for us to do than play golf and travel to Florida. The so-called retirement years are great times to go on Mission trips, give more time to your church, and minister to the needy in your community. Let's be more concerned with eternal investments than our investments toward retirement. We can't take our riches with us. Our large barns will not gain us eternal life, and they will burn away with all other wood, hay, and stubble in the life to come.[231]

The fool believed he was in charge of his own destiny and that bigger barns would bring satisfaction. He didn't believe God would hold him accountable for his actions and attitudes. Therefore, he sold his soul to build bigger barns and enjoy temporary worldly temptations.

Invest in Your Soul

Jesus' second financial principle is: we should be rich toward God. We must be more concerned about the quality of our soul than the equity of our assets. For "the world is passing away, and also its lusts, but the one who does the will of God will abide forever."[232]

Paul beautifully summarized Jesus' first two financial principles, not hoarding wealth and being rich toward God, with these words:

> But godliness actually is a means of great gain, when accompanied by contentment. For we have brought nothing into the world, so we cannot take anything out of it either. And if we have food and covering, with these we shall be content. But those who want to get rich fall into temptation and a snare and many foolish and harmful desires which plunge men into ruin and destruction. For the love of money is a root of all sorts of evil, and some by longing for it have wandered away from the faith, and pierced themselves with many a pang. But flee from these things, you man of God; and pursue righteousness, godliness, faith, love, perseverance and gentleness.[233]

Don't be a fool! Don't hoard your wealth! Invest in your soul. Invest in the things of God. Scripture says the fool is the one who invests his treasure only for himself.[234]

God will Provide

After the parable, Jesus reminded His disciples that God will provide for those who are rich toward Him.

> And He said to His disciples, "For this reason I say to you, don't be anxious for your life, as to what you shall eat; nor for your body, as to what you shall put on. For life is more than food, and the body than clothing (Luke 12:22)."

We are rich toward God when we commit our lives to His service and give toward His work. When we do this, God will meet our needs. Jesus explained this principle through the illustration of creation.

> Consider the ravens, for they neither sow nor reap; and they have no storeroom nor barn; and yet God feeds them; how much more valuable you are than the birds! And which of you by being anxious can add a single cubit to his life's span? If then you can't do even a very little thing, why are you anxious about other matters? Consider the lilies, how they grow; they neither toil nor spin; but I tell you, even Solomon in all his glory did not clothe himself like one of these. But if God so arrays the grass in the field, which is alive today and tomorrow is thrown into the furnace, how much more will He clothe you, O men of little faith! And don't seek what you shall eat, and what you shall drink, and don't keep worrying. For all these things the nations of the world eagerly seek; but your Father knows that you need these things (Luke 12:24-30).

We are not to be wrapped in worry concerning material things. God doesn't want us losing sleep over unnecessary debt.[235] God doesn't want us getting ulcers as we go through bankruptcy. But if God is going to provide for our needs, we must submit to the principles of His Word. This doesn't mean we shouldn't seek income or have a productive job. It does mean we shouldn't focus our attention on material possessions or financial wealth. We are to focus instead on spiritual possessions. Are we growing in our relationship with Christ, or are we only looking for business relationships? Do we spend time with God in prayer and in the

Word, or do early morning business meetings snuff out our time with Him? Are we involved in the life of the church, or do we work so many hours we have no time for fellowship groups or prayer meetings? If we are rich toward God, we will give our lives for people and things of eternal value.

Financial Giving

The third financial principle Jesus gave is: we should be rich toward God's work. Jesus told His disciples, "Sell your possessions and give to charity; make yourselves purses which do not wear out, an unfailing treasure in heaven, where no thief comes near, nor moth destroys."[236]

Before we jump to conclusions, let us remember that God called the disciples, a special group, to follow Jesus as itinerant evangelists, a special task. They needed no earthly possessions because God provided their needs through those they met. As they invested their lives in this specific ministry, people came to faith in Jesus Christ. Healing came to the diseased. The truth of the gospel spread throughout the world. What an incredible return on the disciples' investment! God doesn't ask all Christians to sell all of their possessions, but He does call them to give Him their lives. We are to ask, "What has God called me to do? How am I to invest my life?"[237]

Paul wrote about how to invest our riches in 1 Timothy 6:17-19. After stating that contentment comes from seeking the things of God,[238] he writes,

> Instruct those who are rich in this present world not to be conceited or to fix their hope on the uncertainty of riches, but on God, who richly supplies us with all things to enjoy. Instruct them to do good, to be rich in good works, to be generous and ready to share,

> storing up for themselves the treasure of a good foundation for the future, so that they may take hold of that which is life indeed.

We too often think of ourselves as owners of possessions when we are only stewards. Everything we have belongs to God. The parable of the talents in Matthew 25 reminds us of this sobering truth. God will hold us accountable for all He has given us, including our money.

Humble Giving

Proverbs 3:5-10 explains one way we can humble ourselves financially.

> Trust in the Lord with all your heart,
> And do not lean on your own understanding.
> In all your ways acknowledge Him,
> And He will make your paths straight.
> Do not be wise in your own eyes;
> Fear the Lord and turn away from evil.
> It will be healing to your body,
> And refreshment to your bones.
> Honor the Lord from your wealth,
> And from the first of all your produce;
> So your barns will be filled with plenty,
> And your vats will overflow with new wine.

If we are truly going to trust God and not be wise in our own eyes financially, then we will give back to God a portion of our income. This is not to be done out of what we have left over at the end of the month. We are to give to Him as soon as we receive income from Him. As we have seen in the promise of Proverbs 3, God will supply our needs as we honor and trust Him by giving to His work.

Many people believe that all Christians, no matter what their income, should give at least a tenth of their income to the work of God. Even though this specific principle is not mentioned in the New Testament, it seems to be assumed by the early church.[239] The key principle for giving to God's work in the New Testament is found in 2 Corinthians 9:7, "Let each one do just as he has purposed in his heart; not grudgingly or under compulsion; for God loves a cheerful giver."[240] God wants us to give with hilarity.[241] He wants us to laugh with worshipful joy as we give to His work. It doesn't please God for us to give with a proud attitude; He would rather have the widow's mite.[242] It doesn't please God when we give only to gain a plaque on the wall of our church building;[243] He would rather have an anonymous one-dollar gift. How often are you smiling when you put your money in the offering basket? We are to give to God financially as a humble act of worship, recognizing with thanksgiving and cheerfulness that all we have is His.

Martin Luther once said, "There are three conversions: the conversion of the heart, the mind, and the purse."[244] Jesus concluded in Luke 12, "For where your treasure is, there will your heart be also."[245]

Our hearts should primarily seek God and His kingdom, and the greatest representative of His kingdom is the local church. Humble believers who submit their lives to the Word of God will give to God's work through the local church. Some believe we should give at least 10 percent of our income to our local church, yet not all local churches are worthy of it.[246] Is your church a good steward of its financial resources? Is it truly helping fulfill the Great Commission? If it is, maybe you should consider giving more to the work of God through your local church. If it's not, maybe you should consider changing churches.[247]

We can give to God's work not only through the local church, but through Christian organizations and individuals.

We may do this through our own church's missions budget or on an individual basis. There are advantages and disadvantages to both. Missions committees can protect our investments. They can verify missionaries' training and the organizations' integrity in ministry. A dynamic committee will create personal involvement in a congregation through regularly updating information about the church's missions work and by challenging people to write, pray, and give to these ministries. Some prefer the personal touch of giving to missionaries or ministries directly. Whatever our preference, we should be giving to the work of missions.

We can also give to God's work through meeting the needs of people. This may include giving to people and causes that are not exclusively Christian. However, our priority must be for our brothers and sisters in Christ and for spreading the gospel.[248]

If you want to support the community through public television or medical charities, please don't give impulsively—not even to a needy person on the street. As much as possible, we should work from a budget. This will help us be good stewards of the resources God has given to us. Prayerfully consider what you are currently giving to the work of God. Then if you feel the freedom, budget additional giving for unplanned charities (these may be friends, people on the street, community needs, or other Christian organizations). Just be careful about giving to organizations that work against the cause of Christ.[249]

There is much confusion about how we are to handle our money today.[250] But God tells us to be good overseers of all He has given to us. In fact, God challenged the Israelites to test Him in their giving. "Bring the whole tithe into the storehouse ... and test Me now in this, ... if I will not open for you the windows of heaven, and pour out for you a blessing until it overflows" (Malachi 3:10). Let us trust God with all we have. Let us apply the principles of not hoarding money, being rich toward God, and being rich toward God's work. As we focus on God and His kingdom with our resources, we know God will provide for our needs that we might serve Him all the more.

A Suggested Prayer:

Lord, I confess I have not been a humble steward with the resources You have entrusted to me. Far too often I think of what I have as my own. Far too often I seek to gain greater wealth for my own pleasure, rather than being rich toward You, Your people and Your endeavors. Thank You for allowing me to enjoy the resources I have, and give me wisdom in managing them. Help me to humbly manage what You have loaned to me that more people would grasp Your grace and glory. In Jesus' name. Amen.

Chapter 13

The Exaltation of Humility

Chuck Colson sat on a platform, waiting his turn to speak to the inmates who had gathered. His mind wandered to the many successes he had achieved in his life—awards, positions, the American Dream. Colson had achieved all this world had to offer and yet concluded this:

> My life of success was not what made this morning so glorious—all my achievements meant nothing in God's economy. No, the real legacy of my life was my biggest failure—that I was an ex-convict. My greatest humiliation—being sent to prison—was the beginning of God's greatest use of my life; He chose the one experience in which I could not glory for His glory.... Only when I lost everything I thought made Chuck Colson a great guy had I found the true self God intended me to be and the true purpose of my life.[251]

Only when we truly humble ourselves before God will He exalt us.[252] The idea of the humble being exalted has always been an intriguing one for me. As we previously discussed, the humble person is one who wants to forget about self and do all for God's glory. The humble person walks in submissive obedience to God. Discipleship leader Jack Mayhall wrote, "Humility simply doesn't think of itself at all—but of Christ."[253] But why, when we finally stop thinking of ourselves, does God seemingly add to our dilemma by exalting us?

We find this paradox in many Bible passages.[254] The Apostle James exhorted believers that their selfishness and lusts were creating problems in the church. Their desire to be friends with the world made them enemies of God. Such people had to quit riding the fence. They were living a double life. They must fully give their lives over to the Almighty. Not doing so was prideful. James wrote,

> But He gives a greater grace. Therefore it says, "God is opposed to the proud, but gives grace to the humble."[255] Submit therefore to God. Resist the devil and he will flee from you. Draw near to God and He will draw near to you. Cleanse your hands, you sinners; and purify your hearts, you double-minded. Be miserable and mourn and weep; let your laughter be turned into mourning, and your joy to gloom. Humble yourselves in the presence of the Lord, and He will exalt you.[256]

If we are going to experience the full grace of God, we must humble ourselves. James gave a synopsis on how to do that: submit to God. Acknowledge who God is and who you are. Recognize His greatness and power, and your limited nature. Then choose actively to obey Him.

Submissive obedience is true humility. But we must also renounce the devil. We should not only believe in a personal devil, but we should also reject who he is and all he stands for.[257] In the early church, this renunciation was taken literally. During one's baptism, as if speaking to the devil, the candidate said boldly, "I renounce thee, Satan, and all thy service and all thy works."[258]

True repentance and submission to God will cause us to flee from evil and the evil one. We often tinker with sin. We watch programs on television that add to our impurities. We walk around the mall waiting to be tempted by unnecessary purchases.[259] Instead, we must hate evil and cling to what is good.[260] Each of us needs to ask, "What must I do to resist the devil in my life?"

Also, the text in James tells us we must be sober in spirit, not laughing at sin and impurity, but seriously considering how God wants us to walk in holiness. Pastor and best-selling author Kent Hughes states,

> [This passage] is a scathing denunciation of Christians who are so insensitive and superficial that they are laughing when they ought to be weeping! Some laughter indicates a sickness of soul which only tears can cure. Have we wept over our sins?[261]

Only when we submit to God, resist the devil, and turn from sin (James 4:6-10) are we ready to humble ourselves before God. How long has it been since you spent time alone with God, asking Him to reveal your sin and purify your soul? We can be praised by the world without this practice, but God will never exalt us until we come before Him with an honest heart.

He Exalts the Humble

What does it mean that God will exalt us? "Exalt" means

"to lift up, to raise up." I find two possible applications for our lives. The most obvious is that we will be exalted to eternal life.[262] I will discuss this in the next chapter. But the context of James 4 and 1 Peter 5, along with other passages, leads me to believe God may exalt the humble in this life. When we are crucified with Christ and humble ourselves before Almighty God, He shows us true meaning in life. Jesus said, "The thief comes only to steal, kill, and destroy; I came that they might have life, and have it abundantly" (John 10:10).[263] Proverbs 22:4 states, "The reward of humility and the fear of the Lord are riches, honor, and life." God wants Christians to live life to the fullest. He wants us to know peace and contentment in the middle of chaos. The Christian life is to be the most adventurous, exciting, and joyous life a person can live. So why are many believers walking around with frowns and slumped shoulders rather than smiles and straight backs? Why are many in the church lacking contentment and fulfillment? It's because they aren't walking in humility. "And what does the LORD require of you but to do justice, to love kindness, and to walk humbly with your God?"[264] Many today are relying upon their own insights and strength rather than rejoicing in the freedom God gives as we walk humbly according to His will. God wants to exalt us, to lift us above the mundane.

Exalted by Others

As we humble ourselves before God, He will exalt us before others. The life of Joseph is a beautiful example of this principle. His brothers sold him into slavery. Potiphar's[265] wife wrongly accused him of rape. The cupbearer forgot him in jail. Yet in spite of his difficulties, Joseph continued to trust God. God exalted him in Potiphar's house. "And the Lord was with Joseph, so he became a successful man"

(Genesis 39:2). God exalted Joseph in jail. "The chief jailer did not supervise anything under Joseph's charge because the LORD was with him; and whatever he did, the LORD made to prosper" (Genesis 39:23). And after correctly interpreting Pharaoh's dream, Joseph became a ruler over Egypt. God exalted him to a high place of authority. As Joseph continued to humble himself before God, in spite of calamities, God raised him to save the land of Egypt and provide for his own family in the time of famine. Even when he reflected upon the incredible calamity of being sold into slavery by his brothers, Joseph recognized the hand of God upon his life. Following the death of his father, Joseph humbly said to his brothers, "… you meant evil against me, but God meant it for good in order to bring about this present result, to preserve many people alive."[266] As we humble ourselves before God, he will exalt us before others, so that we might in turn exalt Him.

God can even exalt us in times of calamity. None of us want tragedy in our lives. We shirk away from the responsibility and heartache it brings. But as we accept God's work in our lives, or what God allows, we can truly believe "… that God causes all things to work together for good to those who love God, to those who are called according to His purpose."[267] As we trust God, others will see Jesus in our lives and be drawn to Him.

Whether in good times or bad, our desire should be to exalt God in everything we do. Jesus said in Matthew 5:16, "Let your light shine before men in such a way that they may see your good works, and glorify your Father who is in heaven."

Few who saw will ever forget baseball great Orel Hershiser looking heavenward after the final pitch of the 1988 World Series. Hershiser had set all kinds of pitching records that year, and had become a world champion. Later, Hershiser sang the doxology on Johnny Carson's late-night talk show, just as he often did in the dugout. God exalted this humble man in the eyes of the world that He might be exalted Himself.

But Hershiser faced tough times in his baseball career. After thirteen months of painful rehabilitation following shoulder surgery in 1990, he said,

> There are probably more people going through tough times than there are people who have their life under control. If I can show that God is faithful through tough times, that's a statement and testimony of His power. He can carry me through it and He can carry anybody through the tough times that they might be having.[268]

As you give yourself wholly to God, your life will be a testimony to others. They will see Christ in you and be drawn to Him. They may do you favors. They may put you in high positions because of your integrity and character. They may ask why you are joyous and content in the midst of tough circumstances. They will respect you for your unending perseverance and stalwart faith. God will use you to draw others to Himself.

Exalting Ourselves

As we humble ourselves before God, we will be exalted by ourselves. Let us remember we are not talking about deification. In Chapter 11, we found as we spend time in the presence of God, we will recognize we are unworthy sinners deserving eternal separation from God. We know He alone is the One we should please. He alone is worthy of our praise, full exaltation, and worship.[269]

Yet because of God's grace and mercy, we are now precious in His eyes and usable for His glory. We can be thankful for who we are in Jesus Christ. We have received His adoption as sons and daughters, spiritual blessings, grace, and a rich inheritance.[270] How special we are because God gave us His image, His gifts, and His Son. As we discussed in Chapter 11, when we humble ourselves before God, we gain a proper perspective concerning who we are in Jesus Christ. Therefore, it's appropriate to say we become exalted in our own eyes.

Exalted by Him

Many Scriptures show that God wants to exalt and bless us as we trust our lives to Him.[271] A well-known passage is "and if My people who are called by My name humble themselves and pray, and seek My face and turn from their wicked ways, then I will hear from heaven, will forgive their sin, and will heal their land" (2 Chronicles 7:14). God will hear those who sincerely come to Him with repentant hearts, ready to submit their lives to Him. They will be lifted up and He will bless their lives.

To the Hebrew nation, land was important and symbolic. God often gave land or took it away based on Israel's obedience.[272] When God says He will heal their land as a response to their humility, He is promising to bless the nation when they turn to Him.

Likewise, when we come before God in humility, He will bless us. This doesn't necessarily mean financial or material blessing. But Scripture is clear God will give us abundance in our hearts.

> You younger men, likewise, be subject to your elders; and all of you, clothe yourselves with humility toward one another, for God is opposed to the proud, but gives grace to the humble. Humble yourselves, therefore, under the mighty

> hand of God, that He may exalt you at the proper time, casting all your anxiety upon Him, because He cares for you (1 Peter 5:5-7).[273]

We don't need to be worried. We need not be anxious. As we come before God, He will grant us peace. Paul exhorted, "Be anxious for nothing, but in everything by prayer and supplication with thanksgiving let your requests be made known to God. And the peace of God, which surpasses all comprehension, shall guard your hearts and your minds in Christ Jesus" (Philippians 4:6, 7). If we carry our burdens on our shoulders, we haven't carried them to the cross. Freedom from anxiety over a project at work, freedom from worry over finances, freedom from unease about our children's safety—this sounds like the abundant life!

Second Chronicles 16:9 also teaches God wants to exalt us. "For the eyes of the LORD move to and fro throughout the earth that He may strongly support those whose heart is completely His." God is looking for a few good men and women. Men and women who will give Him their whole hearts that He might encourage, strengthen, and bless them for His glory.

David Brainerd was such a man. His life was short, only twenty-nine years. His mission to the Indians of New Jersey and Pennsylvania in the early 1700's lasted only four years. Yet, in the midst of physical weakness and discouragement in ministry, Brainerd continued to trust and seek God. His private journal entry of September 8, 1744, shows his constant yearning to know and love God.

> In the evening God was pleased to assist me in prayer, and give me freedom at the throne of grace. My soul was so engaged and enlarged in the sweet exercise, that I spent an

> hour in it, and knew not how to leave the mercy seat. Oh, how I delighted to pray and cry to God! I saw that God was both able and willing to do all that I desired for myself, and His church in general. I was likewise much enlarged and assisted in family prayer. Afterwards, when I was just going to bed, God helped me to renew my petition, with ardor and freedom. Oh, it was to me a blessed evening of prayer! Bless the Lord, O my soul![274]

Devoted monk, Brother Lawrence, declared, "Let Him do what He pleases with me; I desire only Him, and to be wholly devoted to Him."[275] We need men and women who will cast off the world and put on Jesus Christ. We need men and women today whose hearts are fully God's.

As Canadian homemaker Fern Nichols' two sons entered junior high school in the fall of 1984, she felt burdened to pray for them. She asked God to give her one other mom to join in intercession. God used her desire for prayer to encourage other moms likewise, and MOMS IN TOUCH began springing up all over British Columbia. From the yearning heart of a devoted mother, God began a ministry that now involves over 100,000 women praying on five different continents.[276]

Andrew Murray said concerning humility, "Water always fills the lowest places first."[277] How might God fill you with His Holy Spirit and exalt you if you submitted your life before His mighty throne? God is looking for people like Fern Nichols. God is looking for people like David Brainerd. God is looking for people like Brother Lawrence. God is looking for people like Orel Hershiser. God is looking for people like Joseph. God is looking for people like Chuck Colson. What does God see when He looks at your heart? Is it completely His? Humble yourself in the presence of the Lord and He will exalt you.

A Suggested Prayer:

Gracious Lord, I seek to fully humbly myself before You. Please, show me any part of my heart that is not completely Yours. Take my life and let it be used completely for Your glory and praise. Help me forget about myself and think only of how I can serve You and follow in the ways of Jesus. If you choose to exalt me in this life, even through my own humiliation or sacrifice, Your will be done. My only desire is to serve my King. In Jesus' glorious name, Amen.

Chapter 14

The Victory of Humility

"I have nothing to offer."

That's what Los Angeles Dodger's star outfielder Kirk Gibson told coach Tommy Lasorda. Gibson didn't even bother to suit up. Why should he when his legs hurt so much he couldn't run or push off in the batter's box?

The Dodgers' situation looked grim as they faced the Oakland A's in the first game of the 1988 World Series. Gibson's situation looked grim as he sat in the cave of the training room. Feeling discouraged, he watched the game on television while his teammates went out for the introductions.

By the seventh inning, the Dodgers were down 4-3. Dodger announcer Vin Scully, in his legendary voice, speculated about possible Dodger pinch hitters in the final innings. He mentioned Gibson's unavailability, which riled Gibson. "Who says I can't hit?" Gibson sneered, and he started dressing.

By the eighth inning, Gibson made his way to the underground batting cages, attempting his painful swing on a practice tee. In the ninth, Gibson sent the bat boy to tell Lasorda to meet him in the runway. "I think I can hit for you," Gibson told his coach. Lasorda decided that if anyone reached base, he would call Gibson to step to the plate.

It happened. With two outs, the A's walked pinch-hitter Mike Davis intentionally. Davis had played for the A's the previous year and they feared his power. The A's also knew the Dodger bench was weak.

Then out of the dugout came Kirk Gibson. Dodger stadium went bananas. Determination exuded from Gibson's face. The drama was unbelievable. But on the first pitch, Gibson looked woeful. He almost fell over, barely getting a piece of the pitch for a foul ball. At his next attempt, Gibson fouled off another. On the third pitch, he lunged at the ball and dribbled it down the first base line. As he pitifully hobbled down to first, the ball rolled foul. Gibson didn't swing at the next pitch and Mike Davis stole second without drawing a throw. The next two pitches from Dennis Eckersly, the A's ace, were balls. What a scene! A 3-2 count. The tying run on second ... the winning run at the plate ... the bottom of the ninth in the first game of the World Series! Yet, the hero, Kirk Gibson, could barely walk. He didn't seem to have a chance. The next pitch would change baseball history.[278]

The Greatest Drama

There was a more dramatic scene about 2,000 years ago. It didn't take place in a baseball stadium, but on a hill. The hero of many, Jesus the Nazarene, had been beaten beyond recognition and now faced the brutal death of crucifixion. Roman soldiers nailed Him to a cross and then lowered the beam into Golgotha's soil between two thieves. Jesus had done nothing worthy of death. Yet as He gasped for breath, He prayed for the forgiveness of those who unjustly punished Him.

Finally it ended. At three in the afternoon on that fateful Friday, Jesus Christ died. The veil of the temple was torn from top to bottom. Lightning flashed as God's pain and wrath came forth in a thunderous roar. Jesus' disciples were stunned. His followers were numb. Many hoped Jesus would overthrow the tyrannical Romans and bring in God's kingdom. But He died. He didn't have a heart attack or die of old age. Jesus died as a criminal, as one accursed of God.

Before the Sabbath began, Joseph of Arimathea and Nicodemus asked governor Pilate for Jesus' body that they might give Him a proper burial. They took Jesus only a short way from the ominous hill of Golgotha and placed Him in a new garden tomb. What sorrow these men and the other disciples felt as the curse of death bruised their Hero. The One who had promised deliverance to others needed it Himself.

It didn't look good for the disciples. It didn't look good for Christianity. It didn't look good for Jesus. The Son of God was dead!

Good Friday and the death of Jesus are where we started this book on humility. Christ's death is the greatest example of humility ever given. Philippians 2:8 reads, "And being found in appearance as a man He humbled Himself by becoming obedient to the point of death, even death on the cross." Throughout these pages, we have talked about our need to die to self, to be crucified with Christ, and to live in submissive obedience to the Word and will of God.

But what is the result of our obedience? What happens when we choose to follow the way and will of God?

What was the result of the death of Jesus? Life. Easter morning resulted from Golgatha. The resurrection resulted from His crucifixion. Exaltation resulted from His humiliation.

> Therefore *(because of His submissive obedience to the will of His Father)* also God highly exalted Him, and bestowed on Him the name which is

> above every name, that at the name of Jesus every knee should bow, of those who are in heaven, and on earth, and under the earth, and that every tongue should confess that Jesus Christ is Lord, to the glory of God the Father (Philippians 2:8, emphasis mine).

Only through His crucifixion and death did exaltation come. Only through being accursed by God for humanity's sin did exaltation come. Only through being separated from the Father for the first time did His rightful exaltation to God's right hand come.[279]

Exalted by His Resurrection

Because Jesus humbled Himself to the point of death, God exalted Him through the resurrection. God foretold that Messiah would rise from the dead.[280] Jesus predicted that He would rise on the third day.[281] Jesus' resurrection proved His claims to be the Son of God. In Luke 24:44-47, Jesus explained the importance of these events in fulfilling Old Testament prophecies. Later, Peter emphasized that the resurrection of Christ would help all "know for certain that God has made Him both Lord and Christ—this Jesus whom you crucified" (Acts 2:22-36).[282]

It's one thing to *say* that Michael Jordan is the best player to ever play in the National Basketball Association. Some people just like the way Mike slam dunks and therefore their emotions may get the best of them in their debates. However, it's another thing to back up one's argument by looking at the facts. Jordan led the NBA in scoring for ten years, was elected to the all-defensive team eight years, and led his team, the Chicago Bulls, to six World Championships. These are only a few of the plethora of statistics which support the claim that Michael Jordan is the best basketball player in the history of the game. He even made it to the NBA All-Star game as a Washington Wizard! The videos of his slam dunks and last second game-winning shots aren't bad either.

The resurrection of Jesus is the final evidence that Jesus is the Son of God. His teachings, miracles, and fulfilled prophecies also support this claim. No sane person would believe that martyred cult leader David Koresh of Waco, Texas was actually the Son of God. His temperament and actions made that claim ludicrous. But there is plenty of evidence from the life of Jesus that would point to His authenticity. Yes, the resurrection highly exalts Jesus.

Exalted by His Ascension

Because Jesus humbled Himself to the point of death, He was also exalted through the ascension. God raised Jesus to His rightful place at the right hand of God. He returned to His throne which He left when He departed heaven and became a man. Peter spoke of Christ's ascension as exalting the Messiah. "Therefore having been exalted to the right hand of God, ..." (Acts 2:33). In this position of authority and power, He now reigns and intercedes for the saints.[283] Theologian Wayne Grudem writes the ascension "shows both the completion of Christ's work of redemption and reception of new authority as God-man to reign over the universe."[284] His ascension to the right hand of the Father highly exalts Jesus.

Exalted by His Return

Finally, because Jesus humbled Himself to the point of death, He will be exalted at His return. This seems to be Paul's main point in Philippians 2:9-11. The Father lifted the Son to honor through His resurrection and ascension. Christ's name is now above every name. But not everyone today recognizes Jesus as Lord.

Some today call Muhammad or Buddha lord. Others call their jobs or egos lord. But when Christ comes again in glory, every knee will bow. It will not matter if people previously acknowledged Christ as Lord or if they like it or not. All will acknowledge Jesus Christ at that time as the King of kings and Lord of lords.[285] Because Jesus humbled Himself to the point of death on the cross, He was highly exalted through His resurrection and ascension. He will be highly exalted at His imminent return.

We will be Exalted

In the previous chapter we learned God will exalt us in this life as we humble ourselves. As we live in submissive obedience, He will give us peace, joy, and contentment because of our position in Christ. But also, through the death and resurrection of Jesus Christ, we know that those who humble themselves in this life will be exalted with Jesus for all of eternity.

Because of His resurrection, we are assured that one day, hopefully very soon, we will rise to meet Him in the air. "The dead in Christ shall rise first. Then we who are alive and remain shall be caught up together with them."[286] We will be together for all eternity. Paul writes,

> If Christ is not raised, we are to be counted as fools. For if the dead are not raised, not even Christ has been raised; and if Christ has not been raised, your faith is worthless; you are still in your sins. Then those also who have fallen asleep in Christ have perished. If we have hoped in Christ in this life only, we are of all men most to be

> pitied. But now Christ has been raised from the dead, the first fruits of those who are asleep. For since by a man came death, by a man also came the resurrection of the dead. For as in Adam all die, so also in Christ all shall be made alive. But each in his own order: Christ the first fruits, after that those who are Christ's at His coming, then comes the end, when He delivers up the kingdom to the God and Father, when He has abolished all rule and all authority and power. For He must reign until He has put all His enemies under His feet (1 Corinthians 5:16-25).[287]

His resurrection and exaltation are our hope. True believers in Jesus Christ will be exalted in eternity regardless of this life's circumstances. Believers have the promise of heaven. Be assured that when I mention believers in Jesus, I don't mean knowing about Jesus Christ historically or intellectually. I am saying that those who know Christ personally and have sincerely asked Him to pay for the penalty of their sins have eternal hope in the life to come.

Our Eternal Home

A wealthy young man was about to die. He had not anticipated his death, as almost no one does, so he sent for his lawyer to make a will. He wanted his wife and child to have the home. He explained to his little girl, "Honey, this piece of paper will assure that you and Mommy will have this house to live in, even though I have to leave." But the little girl didn't understand death. She stood near and said, "Papa, have you got a home in that land to which you are going?" But the wealthy young father had no answer, for he had not asked Jesus to prepare a home for him.[288]

Has Christ built a home in heaven for you? He is preparing dwelling places for all believers so we will be with Him for eternity.[289] Our resurrection bodies will not decay.[290] We will walk on streets of pure gold in the New Jerusalem.[291] There will be no more pain, no more tears, no more mourning, for these things will have passed away.[292] We will be lifted up, exalted beyond the cares and fears of this world, with Jesus Christ. The victory will be ours.

Humble yourselves before God, and hold firmly to the exaltation of heaven. This life brings difficulty and pain. The flesh and sin engage us in agonizing battle.[293] Evil powers seek to destroy us.[294] But one day we will truly be exalted into newness of life as we will stand in Christ's resurrected, exalted presence.

The Victory of Humility

The final pitch was thrown. Gibson lunged as if possessed by power beyond himself and a sensational roar sounded from the crowd. The ball jumped off the bat. The sphere seemed to be propelled by an angel as it sailed over the right field fence to win the game. Gibson jubilantly threw a fist of victory into the air as he rounded first base. Though it had not looked good for the Dodgers, their fans, or Gibson, he won the victory.

On Good Friday, things didn't look good for Jesus. It didn't look good for the disciples. It didn't look good for you and me. Our Redeemer had been bruised, yet He was about to crush the head of His enemy.[295] God raised Him from the dead and exalted Him in glory. He won the victory over sin and death.

If we'll put our trust and faith in God, submitting our lives in humility before His throne of grace, we too, will gain the victory through humility. Heaven, and His presence, is our real reward. He is the final victory of humility.

A Suggested Prayer:

Oh, Lord, my full confidence is in Your death and resurrection. I praise You, that because of Your payment for my sins, You will exalt me when my time on earth is done. I will be with You for all eternity. Hallelujah! Help me to further be ready to stand before You by living each day in submissive obedience to You in every aspect of my life. I love You, O Sovereign and Holy King. In Jesus' name, Amen.

Prologue

In the year of King Uzziah's death, I saw the Lord sitting on a throne, lofty and exalted, with the train of His robe filling the temple. Seraphim stood above Him, each having six wings; with two he covered his face, and with two he covered his feet, and with two he flew. And one called out to another and said,

"Holy, Holy, Holy, is the LORD of hosts,
The whole earth is full of His glory."

And the foundations of the thresholds trembled at the voice of him who called out, while the temple was filling with smoke. Then I said,

"Woe is me, for I am ruined!
Because I am a man of unclean lips,
And because I live among a people of unclean lips;
For my eyes have seen the King, the LORD of hosts."

> Then one of the seraphim flew to me, with a burning coal in his hand which he had taken from the altar with tongs. And he touched my mouth with it and said, "Behold, this has touched your lips; and your iniquity is taken away, and your sin is forgiven" (Isaiah 6:1-7).

What an awesome sight for Isaiah as the glory of God surrounded him! There sat the Lord, high and exalted, on His throne. The brilliance and majesty of His robe's train filled the temple.[296] Winged creatures cried back and forth to one another, "Holy, Holy, Holy, is the LORD of hosts, the whole earth is full of His glory." The foundations of the temple rattled and filled with smoke.

How did Isaiah respond? Did he rush into God's open arms? Did he telephone his neighbors? Did he issue a statement to the press? No. Isaiah responded by confessing his sins and the sins of his people. Isaiah was in the most humbling position any one can achieve—in the presence of God.

And how did God respond? Did He wipe out Isaiah because of His sins? Did He cast him into hell as punishment? Did He command Isaiah to wash out his mouth because it was unclean? No. God met Isaiah's need. He sent His messenger to touch Isaiah's place of impurity with a burning coal. The seraphim told Isaiah, "your iniquity is taken away, and your sin is forgiven."

We don't need to fear humbling ourselves in the presence of God. We can't run from Him. He already knows our sins. Let us seek Him with all our hearts and desire His forgiveness, fellowship and glory. When we humble ourselves in His iridescent presence, He doesn't cast us aside. He meets our greatest need—forgiveness. He provides the burning coal for our sins through His Son at Calvary.

What happened to Isaiah after he humbled himself

before God and received cleansing? Isaiah was ready to fulfill the mission for his life. The voice of the Lord called out, "Whom shall I send, and who will go for Us?" Isaiah immediately responded, "Here am I. Send me!"

The great American theologian Jonathan Edwards said, "Nothing sets a person so much out of the devil's reach as humility, and so prepares the mind for true divine light without darkness, and so clears the eye to look on things as they truly are…."[297]

Many believers today miss out on God's plan for them because they aren't willing to humble themselves before Him. They are unwilling to walk in submissive obedience to the Almighty King. As A. W. Tozer writes, "Every soul belongs to God and exists by His pleasure. God being Who and What He is, and we being who and what we are, the only thinkable relation between us is one of full lordship on His part and complete submission on ours."[298]

To know the joy of obedience, we must come into God's presence and submit to Him. Only then does God fill us with His Spirit and provide meaning in life that brings joy and abundance. This doesn't mean life will be easy. But God will bless us as we make our lives available to Him.

Let our burning passion be to please God and be used for His glory. "Humble yourselves, therefore, under the mighty hand of God, that He might exalt you at the proper time, casting all your anxiety upon Him, because He cares for you."[299] Walk in humility toward your loving heavenly Father and you will know the joy of obedience.

A Suggested Prayer:

Almighty King, I continue to humble myself under Your mighty hand. Mold and make me into a vessel for Your honor and glory. Let my burning passion be to please and honor You in every aspect of my life. Here I am, O Lord, send me. Enable me to walk in humility for Your glory. In Jesus' name, Amen.

Notes

1 Andrew Murray, Humility, Whitaker House, Springdale, Pennsylvania, 1982, p. 13.
2 Richard Baxter, The Reformed Pastor, ed. by William Brown, The Banner of Truth Trust, Carlisle, Pennsylvania, reprint, 1989, p.146.
3 Information taken from www.theenolagay.com
4 Romans 3:23-24; 6:23
5 Many testified of the holiness of Jesus, including Jesus Himself. From the gospels of Luke and John we find these references: Luke 4:34; 23:40-12, 47; John 7:18; 8:46; 9:24-25; 19:6
6 The word for grasped is *arpagmos*- According to Thayer's this word means to seize or rob. Secondarily, it means to be held fast or retained. The second usage seems to be the emphasis in this passage.
7 Philippians 2:7 reads, "but emptied Himself, taking the form of a bondservant, and being made in the likeness of men." The second and third phrase of the verse explain the first phrase, "but emptied Himself." Lightfoot explains, "So far from this: 'he divested Himself,' not of His divine nature, for this was impossible, but 'of the

glories, the prerogatives, of Deity. This He did by taking upon Him the form of a servant.'" J. B. Lightfoot, Paul's Epistle to the Philippians (Zondervan, 1953), p. 112.

Much has been written on this topic. A few suggestions for further study:

Calvin: Institutes of the Christian Religion, Vol. XX, The Library of Christian Classics, ed. John T. McNeill (Philadelphia: The Westminster Press, 1960), p. 476ff.

Alec Motyer, The Message of Philippians: Jesus Our Joy; The Bible Speaks Today: New Testament Commentaries, ed. John R.W. Stott (Downer's Grove, Illinois: InterVarsity Press, 1984), pp. 108-118.

Ralph P. Martin, Philippians, Tyndale New Testament Commentaries, ed. R.G.V. Tasker (Grand Rapids: William B. Eerdmans, 1983), pp. 95-109.

8 The word to empty is *kenoō*. It means to empty, or make void.

9 A.W. Tozer, The Knowledge of the Holy (Bromley, Kent, England: STL Books, 1961) p. 29.

10 Exodus 33:17-23; John 1:18.

11 Isaiah 7:14; Matthew 1:23.

12 Matthew 4.

13 Matthew 20:28; Mark 10:45; Luke 19:10.

14 Hebrews 9:22.

15 This is the apostle Paul's point in Romans 1-3.

16 Romans 3:23; 6:23.

17 Job 2:9-10.

18 Japan's WWII 'no surrender' soldier dies; CNN.com; September 23, 1997.

19 A brief discussion and refutation of Joseph Fletcher's situational ethic is found in chapter 1, "The Crisis in Morality" by Erwin Lutzer of Living Ethically in the 90's, ed. J. Kerby Anderson (Wheaton, Illinois:

Victor Books, 1990). This volume is an excellent resource for other ethical issues discussed in this chapter.

Other helpful volumes concerning situational ethics and social issues are:

R.C. Sproul, Ethics and the Christian (Wheaton, Illinois: Tyndale, 1983).

Cal Thomas, The Death of Ethics in America (Waco, Texas: Word, 1988).

John Jefferson Davis, Evangelical Ethics (Phillipsburg, New Jersey: Presbyterian and Reformed Publishing, 1985).

20 Charles Colson, Against the Night, (Ann Arbor, Michigan: Servant Books, 1989), p. 44.

21 Cal Thomas, The Death of Ethics in America (Waco, Texas: Word Books, 1988), p. 113.

22 "Out of nothing."

23 Psalm 19:1; Romans 1:20.

24 Francis A. Schaeffer, He is There and He Is Not Silent (Wheaton, Illinois: Tyndale House, 1981), p. 77.

25 Carl F. H. Henry, Twilight of a Great Civilization (Westchester, Illinois: Crossway Books, 1988), pp. 21-22.

26 George Barna and Mark Hatch, Boiling Point, (Ventura, California: Regal Books, 2001), pp. 211-219.

27 Ibid., p. 191.

28 John Pollock, John Wesley: Servant of God (Wheaton, Illinois: Victor Books, 1989), p. 87.

29 Ibid., p.97.

30 John 1:1, 2; 14:6; 17:17.

31 Nehemiah 8:10; Psalm 100:1; 132:9; Proverbs 17:22; Matthew 25:21; John 10:10; 16:33; Romans 14:17; Galatians 5:16-26.

32 1 John 5:14-15. A person doesn't necessarily have to go through this process to be empowered by the Spirit.

God knows your heart. But the more specific and honest we can be with God, the better.

33 Billy Graham, The Holy Spirit (Waco, Texas: Word Books, 1978), p. 120.

34 James 1:13.

35 1 Peter 1:14-16.

36 Romans 6:11.

37 Some verses concerning purity are Matthew 15:17-20; Romans 13:14; Philippians 4:8-9; Colossians 3:2; 1 Thessalonians 4:3.

38 I am not saying that watching television itself is wrong or sinful. Like many forms of the media, we must be careful of its influences on our minds and hearts. It has been very helpful to me to dwell upon verses such as Matthew 5:27-29; Romans 12:1-2; Philippians 4:8; 1 Peter 1:13-16; 1 John 2:15-17; and many others in asking God to purify my mind and heart. I also try to ask myself if Jesus would watch this, or would I watch this (read this, listen to this) if Jesus were here with me. Further, would I want my children to watch this? Another possible means to help achieve balance is asking yourself, "Am I spending more time with the media, than I am with God?"

39 We find this struggle to be holy, yet the reality of our sinfulness and the forgiveness of God, in 1 John 1:5 - 2:3.

40 In the April 15, 1993 issue of USA Today, writer Kim Painter reported in the cover story that "only 1% of men say they are gay."

41 Karl Menninger, "Whatever Became of Sin?" (New York: Hawthorne Books, 1973), p. 242.

42 Kim A. Lawson, "Seeking Common Ground," Christianity Today, Vol. 36 (1992), p. 40.

43 1 John 1:9.

44 This will be further discussed in chapter 5.

45 2 Samuel 11:1-12:25

46 2 Samuel 12:9-12; 16:22; 18:14.

47 1 Samuel 13:14; Acts 13:22.

48 Don Baker, Beyond Forgiveness (Portland, Oregon: Multnomah Press, 1984). Praise God that through church discipline this brother was restored.

49 Gary R. Collins, Christian Counseling: A Comprehensive Guide (Waco, Texas: Word Books, 1980), p. 123.

50 Earl D. Wilson, Counseling and Guilt, Resources for Christian Counseling, ed. Gary R. Collins (Waco, Texas: Word Books, 1987), p. 18.

51 Genesis 12:10-20; 20:1-18; Abraham is called a "friend of God" in 2 Chronicles 20:7.

52 Genesis 27. Yet Jacob is blessed by God at Bethel and promised abundance, finally having his name changed to Israel in Genesis 35:9-15.

53 Numbers 20:8-13.

54 John 8:1-11.

55 John 18:15-18, 25-27. Jesus' forgiveness to Peter is implied, first by the character and nature of Jesus, and second by His conversation with Peter in John 21:15-17 where Jesus calls Peter to "tend My sheep."

56 Acts 7:54-8:3; 9:1-22. Again we can assume Christ's forgiveness of Saul through the change in Saul's life and Christ's call upon him. Ephesians 3:1-8 speaks directly of God's grace to Saul (now Paul).

57 1 John 1:9.

58 2 Corinthians 5:21.

59 1 Peter 3:18. I encourage you to spend some time meditating upon the promise and wonder of God's forgiveness toward you. Here are some other Scriptures confirming that God loves you and offers His forgiveness to you. In no way is this list exhaustive, but they are some of my favorites. Genesis 3:21;

1 Samuel 12:13; 2 Chronicles 30:9; Nehemiah 9:16-17, 30-31; Psalm 51:1-19; 103:10-14; 130:1-8; Isaiah 53; 55:1-7; Lamentations 3:23-32; Matthew 9:11-13; 10:29-31; Luke 15:11-32; 19:1-10; 24:46-47; John 1:29; 3:16; 8:1-11; Acts 10:43; 13:38-39; 16:31-34; Romans 3:23-24; 8:1; 2 Corinthians 8:9; Galatians 1:3-4; Ephesians 2:1-9; Colossians 1:13-14; 2:13-14; Hebrews 9:27-28; Titus 3:5-7; 1 Peter 2:24, 3:18; 1 John 1:9-2:2, 3:16, 4:10.

60 This principle of forgiveness not only applies in our receiving Christ for our salvation, but God's wonderful forgiveness applies to every sin we ever commit. The only unforgivable sin is blasphemy of the Holy Spirit, which I understand to be not allowing the Holy Spirit to minister in your life, i.e., not receiving Christ for salvation (Matthew 12:31-32; Mark 3:28-30; Luke 12:10).

61 John Keegan, The Price of Admiralty (New York: Viking, 1988), pp. 266-267.

62 John 4:34.

63 Isaiah 52:14.

64 "The cross consisted of a perpendicular stake with a crossbeam either at the top of the stake or shortly below the top. The height of the stake was usually little more than the height of a man. A block or a pin was sometimes driven into the stake to serve as a seat for the condemned person, giving partial support to his body. Sometimes also a step for the feet was fixed to the stake. Victims of crucifixion did not usually die for two or three days. But this was determined by the presence or absence of the seat and the foot rest, for a person suspended by his hands lost blood pressure quickly, and the pulse rate was increased. Usually the victim had been severely scourged before crucifixion took place. Total collapse through insufficient blood

circulation to the brain and the heart would follow shortly.

"If the victim could ease his body by supporting himself with the seat and footrest, the blood could be returned to some degree of circulation in the upper part of his body. To fix the hands to the cross beam either cords or nails and cords were used; sometimes the feet were nailed also. When it was desired to bring the torture to an end, the victim's legs were broken below the knees with a club. It was then no longer possible for him to ease his weight, and the loss of blood circulation was accentuated.

"Coronary insufficiency followed shortly. The victim's offense was usually published by a crier who preceded him to the place of execution. Sometimes it was written on a tablet which was carried by the condemned man himself." Parsons Bible Illustrator computer software (Hiawatha, Iowa: Parsons Technology, 1991).

65 Matthew 27:4, Luke 23:13-22; John 9:24-25; 2 Corinthians 5:21; Luke 1:35; Hebrews 7:26; 1 Peter 2:22-24; 1 John 3:9.

66 John 1:29.

67 Some verses that point to this eternal relationship are Genesis 1:26; John 1:1-3; John 8:58; Colossians 1:15-17; and Revelation 22:13.

68 There is much debate about how long Jesus was actually separated from the Father. Some argue that Jesus was separated from the Father for three days between His death and resurrection. It was at this time that He preached the gospel to Old Testament saints, set the captives free from paradise, and upon His resurrection and ascension He led believers who had died into the presence of God the Father. 1 Peter 3:18-20 is interpreted in this way, and His statement on the cross, "It is

finished," only applies to His earthly ministry of paying for the sins of mankind. He still had to experience the separation of hell.

Another view is that Jesus "went through hell" for the three hours of darkness that He was on the cross (Matthew 27:45). His cry "It is finished" points to the fact that all of His earthly ministry and His separation from the Father ended. Matthew 27:52 points to bodies being raised upon Christ yielding His spirit. This verse seems to support the three-hour view. However, either way we understand this doctrine, we know that Christ has won the victory over sin and death through His death and resurrection, however long He was actually separated from the Father.

69 I saw his video. It was awesome. (This story is used with Jim's permission).

70 Matthew 26:45-46.

71 Latin for "the sorrowful road."

72 Matthew 27:39-44.

73 Dietrich Bonhoffer, The Cost of Discipleship, revised and unabridged edition (New York: Collier Books, 1949), p. 342.

74 Norman Grubb, C.T. Studd, Cricketer and Pioneer (Port Washington, Pennsylvania: Christian Literature Crusade, 1933), p. 132.

75 I don't see this statement as meaning three separate actions. Jesus is speaking of the total process of being His disciple. Denying ourselves is a part of taking up our cross (our mission) and following Christ when done in the context of Christian discipleship. At this point we commit ourselves to follow through on whatever God calls us to do. These may be three different mental commitments, but are all essential aspects of following Jesus. We see this in the Garden of Gethsemane in the life of Jesus.

76 Allan Bloom, The Closing of the American Mind (New York: Simon and Schuster, 1987), p. 166.

77 Andrew Murray, The Blessings of Obedience (Springdale, Pennsylvania: Whitaker House, 1984), p. 31.

78 Jerry White, The Power of Commitment (Colorado Springs: Navpress, 1985), p. 18.

79 Information taken from D.L. Moody, The Greatest Evangelist of the Nineteenth Century by Faith Coxe Bailey (Chicago: Moody Press, 1959). The quote is from p. 85.

80 An excellent resource concerning the history of the Bible is The Canon of Scripture by F.F. Bruce (Downer's Grove, Illinois: Inter-varsity Press, 1988).

81 George Gallup, Jr. and Jim Castelli, The People's Religion (New York: Macmillan Publishing Company, 1989), p. 60.

82 Ibid, pp. 60-61. These pages have many interesting statistics on what people in the United States believe about the Bible.

83 George Barna and Mark Hatch, Boiling Point, (Regal Books, Ventura, CA: 2001), p. 211.

84 Ibid., pp. 217-218. Here Barna concurs that eighty percent of the population still believe the Bible is the Word of God, though one out of five believe it is the Word of God, but contains errors.

85 There have been many books written concerning the veracity of the Bible. Here are some of my favorites.

James Montgomery Boice, Foundations of the Christian Faith, rev. ed. (Downer's Grove, Illinois: InterVarsity Press, 1986), pp. 37-98.

Paul Little, Know Why You Believe, expanded by Marie Little (Downer's Grove, Illinois: InterVarsity Press, 1988), pp. 61-99, 113-129.

Josh McDowell, Evidence That Demands a Verdict,

Vol. I, (San Bernardino, California: Here's Life Publishers, 1979), pp. 13-78.

Evangelicals and Inerrancy, ed. Ronald Youngblood (Nashville: Thomas Nelson Publishers, 1984).

B.B. Warfield, The Inspiration and Authority of the Bible (Philadelphia: Presbyterian and Reformed, 1948).

86 Matthew 15:6; 21:42; 22:29; 26:54,56; Mark 7:13; 12:10,24; 14:49; Luke 4:21; 24:27, 45; John 5:39; 7:38,42; 10:35; 13:18; 17:6,12,14,17; 19:28; Acts 1:16.

87 J. Barton Payne lists 113 fulfilled Old Testament prophecies concerning Jesus in his Encyclopedia of Biblical Prophecy (Grand Rapids, Michigan: 1973), pp. 665-8. The following verses include descriptive types and prophecies fulfilled in Jesus the Messiah. Genesis 3:15; 12:3; 17:19; 49:10; Numbers 24:17; Deuteronomy 18:15; Psalm 2:7; 16:10; 22:1, 7, 8; 34:20; 35:11; 41:9; 45:6, 7; 49:15; 68:18; 69:9; 78:2-4; 102:25-27; 109:4; 110:4; Isaiah 9:1, 7, 40:3-5; 53:1, 3, 5, 7, 9, 12; 61:1; Jeremiah 31:15; Daniel 9:25; Hosea 11:1; Micah 5:2; Zechariah 9:9; 11:12; 12:10; Malachi 3:1; 4:5.

88 The terms "Edom" and "Esau" are used interchangeably.

89 International Standard Bible Encyclopedia, Vol. II, (USA: Eerdmans, 1982), p. 20.

90 Isaiah 44:24-45:7

91 Jeremiah 25:12.

92 Gleason L. Archer, Jr., A Survey of the Old Testament Introduction, rev. ed. (Chicago: Moody Press, 1974), p. 371.

93 Luke 21:5-6.

94 A wonderful resource, referred to earlier in footnote 87, is the Encyclopedia of Biblical Prophecy by J. Barton Payne (Grand Rapids: Baker Book House, 1973).

95 "The Word of God" is used in these phrases in the Old Testament: 1 Samuel 9:27; 1 Kings 12:22; 1 Chronicles 17:3; Proverbs 30:5. "Thus says the LORD" is used 481 times in the Old Testament in verses such as Exodus 4:22; Joshua 24:2; and 1 Kings 12:24. "The Word of the LORD" is used 239 times in the Old Testament in verses such as Genesis 15:1; Deuteronomy 34:5; and 1 Kings 16:7. "... the LORD said to me" is used 41 times in the Old Testament in verses such as Deuteronomy 1:42 and Jeremiah 24:3.

96 "The Word of the Lord" is used in 15 places in the New Testament, such as Luke 12:61; Acts 13:49; 1 Thessalonians 4:15; and 1 Peter 1:25. "The Lord said to me" is used only in Acts 22:10. However, similar phrases are used by Saul (Paul) and Cornelius in Acts 9, 18, 20, 22. "Says the Lord" is used 13 times in the New Testament, such as Acts 7:49; Romans 12:19; 14:11; and Revelation 1:8.

97 "Inspired" literally means "God-breathed."

98 1 Corinthians 2:12, 13; cf. 1 Thessalonians 2:13.

99 Deuteronomy 31:26.

100 2 Chronicles 34-35.

101 F.F. Bruce, <u>The Canon of Scripture</u> (Downer's Grove, Illinois: Intervarsity Press, 1988), pp. 28-29.

102 <u>Early Christian Fathers</u>, ed. Cyril C. Richardson (New York: Collier Books, 1970), p. 109.

103 John Calvin, <u>Institutes of the Christian Religion</u>, ed. John T. McNeill and trans. Ford Lewis Battles (Philadelphia: Westminster Press, 1960), p. 74.

104 I refer you to McDowell, op. cit. Another good resource concerning archeology and inerrancy is <u>God, Revelation, and Authority</u> by Carl F.H. Henry (Waco, Texas: Word Books, 1979), pp. 247, 355ff. These references concerning the findings at Qumran and the Sinai peninsula show that Tiglath-pileser actually did exist.

105 Saint Augustine, Confessions (New York: Viking Penguin Inc, 1961), p. 178.

106 Roland H. Bainton, Here I Stand (New York: Mentor Books, 1977), pp. 49-50.

107 Brother Andrew with John and Elizabeth Sherrill, God's Smuggler (Old Tappan, New Jersey: Fleming H. Revell Company, 1967), p. 42.

108 Romans 10:17.

109 Deuteronomy 6:6-9.

110 Joshua 1:8.

111 These are some examples of commands to listen to and read the Scriptures: Deuteronomy 6:6-9; 10:12-13; 28:13; 31:11-13; 32:46; Joshua 1:8; 8:33-35; 2 Kings 23:2; 2 Chronicles 17:7-9; Nehemiah 8; Psalm 119; Isaiah 34:16; Jeremiah 36:6; Ezekiel 3:10; Luke 11:28; John 8:31-32; 14:21; 15:7, 11; Acts 17:11; 20:32; Romans 12:2; 1 Corinthians 2:12-15; Ephesians 6:17; Colossians 3:16; 2 Timothy 1:13; James 1:21-22; 1 Peter 2:2; 2 Peter 3:2; Jude 17; and Revelation 1:3.

112 Henry H. Halley, Halley's Bible Handbook, Regency Reference Library, 24th edition (Grand Rapids: Zondervan, 1965), p. 4.

113 See the February 15, 1993 issue.

114 Some other verses telling us God will bless us as we read and apply His Word are: Deuteronomy 11; Joshua 1:8; 1 Chronicles 22:13; Psalm 1:1-3; 19:7-11; 37:31; 119; Matthew 7:24-27; 13:23; Luke 11:28; John 8:31-32; 15:7-8; Romans 10:17; Colossians 3:16; 1 Thessalonians 2:13; 2 Timothy 2:15; 2 Timothy 3:15-17; Hebrews 4:12; James 1:22, 2 Peter 1:4; and 1 John 1:4.

115. HOMEADE, Vol. 10, No. 4 (California: Focus on the Family, 1986).

116 This quotation by Samuel Chadwick is taken from the 29th printing of Why Revival Tarries by Leonard

Ravenhill (Minneapolis, Minnesota: Bethany House Publishers, 983), p. 150.

117 John 14:21. This is also discussed in Chapter 8, "The Love of Humility."

118 God desires for us to pray. There are many examples and commands in the Scriptures concerning prayer. 1 Chronicles 16:11; Nehemiah 1:4-11; 2:4; Psalm 116:1-2; 121:1; 123:1; Isaiah 55:6, 7; Jeremiah 33:3; Matthew 5:44; 6:5-12; 7:7-11; John 15:7-8; Acts 1:14; 2:42; Philippians 4:6-7; Colossians 4:2; 1 Timothy 2:8; 1 Thessalonians 5:17.

119 In His humanity, Jesus wanted and needed to pray. Though full of the Spirit, He constantly sought to do the will of the Father (John 4:34). He seems to need the Father's help and support in many situations, such as choosing the twelve apostles (Luke 6:12ff), and before He went to the cross (Luke 22:39-46). He is also setting an example for us in His prayer life (Luke 11:1-13).

120 William Lane translates Mark 1:35, "And in the morning, a great while before day,..." in The Gospel of Mark, The New International Commentary on the New Testament, (Grand Rapids, Michigan: Eerdmans, 1974), p. 80. C.E.B. Cranfield mentions that each time prayer is mentioned concerning Jesus in Mark (here, 6:46, and 14:32ff) it seems to be occurring at dead of night in The Gospel According to St. Mark, The Cambridge Greek Testament Commentary, gen. ed. C.F.D. Moule (Cambridge, England: Cambridge University Press, 1959), pp. 88-89.

121 Psalm 16:11.

122 Hebrews 4:14-16.

123 John 1:12-13; Romans 8:14-17; Galatians 4:4-7.

124 1 Peter 2:9.

125 There are other ways that God gains delight. Here are

some of the verses that speak to this amazing truth: Psalm 37:23; Proverbs 11:1, 20; 12:22; Isaiah 42:1; Isaiah 2:4; Jeremiah 9:23-24; Hosea 6:6; Micah 7:18.

126 Gen. H. Norman Schwarzkopf, <u>It Doesn't Take a Hero</u> (New York: Linda Grey Bantam Books, 1992), p. 412.

127 <u>Newsweek</u> (January 6, 1992, p. 43) reports that even 10 percent of those who don't believe in God, pray daily.

128 George Barna and Mark Hatch, <u>Boiling Point</u> (Ventura, California: Regal Books, a division of Gospel Light, 2001), p. 186.

129 Praise God, He rose again!

130 Pentecost is fifty days after Passover. Traditionally, we understand Jesus was crucified on the day after Passover (Friday), and rose on Sunday. According to Acts 1:3 He appeared for a period of forty days after His resurrection. That would leave seven days between His ascension and Pentecost.

131 Acts 2:42.

132 Romans 8:29-30.

133 Verses that refer to the potter working with the clay: Isaiah 29:16; 45:9; 64:8; Jeremiah 18:1-12; Romans 9:21. Verses that discuss that we will go through discipline, trials, and persecutions: Matthew 5:10-12; Romans 8:18, 33-39; 2 Corinthians 1:1-11; 2 Timothy 3:12; Hebrews 12:11; James 1:2-4. Discipline comes directly from the hand of God. Persecutions and trials are often God sovereignly allowing these things to happen to us. He uses all these things for His glory and our good as we trust in Him.

134 Other examples of the need to pray in times of crises: 1 Kings 8:33; 8:35; 8:48; 2 Chronicles 6:24; 6:26; 6:38; 7:14; Psalm 5:2; 32:6; Jeremiah 29:7, 12; Jonah 1:14.

135 Please note that I am not in opposition to either fund-raising or church growth principles as long as they are used in full dependence upon the power of God and His leading. Some fund-raising tactics create guilt and pressure, rather than Spirit-led giving. Some church growth methods are more a marketing scheme that one throws money at rather than a work of the Holy Spirit. All we do in ministry should be bathed in prayer.

136 Timothy M. Warner, Spiritual Warfare (Wheaton, Illinois: Crossway Books, 991), p. 133. Original quote from Paul Billheimer, Destined for the Throne (Fort Washington, Pennsylvania: Christian Literature Crusade, 1975), p.18.

137 E.M. Bounds, Power through Prayer (Grand Rapids, Michigan: Zondervan Publishing House, 1981), p. 12.

138 Isaiah 6.

139 Acts 9:1-9.

140 Revelation 1:9-20.

141 Isaiah 64:6.

142 2 Corinthians 5:21; 8:9.

143 A few verses to help us meditate upon the attributes of God are: Numbers 11:21-23; Psalm 33; 139:1-6; Isaiah 40; Jeremiah 10:12-16; Romans 11:33; Ephesians 3:20-21; Colossians 1:13-17; 1 Timothy 1:17, Revelation 4:8-11; 5:11-14; 7:9-12.

144 Matthew 7:7-8; James 1:5; 4:2-3.

145 Psalm 37:3-6; Proverbs 3:5-6, Matthew 6:33-34; Philippians 4:6-7.

146 Matthew 6:33-34; Philippians 4:11-19.

147 J.H. Jowett, The Preacher: His Life and Work (New York: Abingdon Press, 1912), p. 66-7.

148 It is not my intention to create a guilt trip for those who for one reason or another can't or don't have a time with God in the morning. You may have an early rising child or some other reason that makes it impos-

sible to lift up your voice to the Lord in the morning. My question then is this: "When do you have your set time with God?" If you have a set time at noon, or when you get home from work, or when the kids take a nap, that's great. But you must have some time that you commit to pour out your heart before His throne. I encourage all of us, including myself, to immediately say a short prayer of commitment to the Lord for the new day as soon as we get up. Then, as soon as possible, spend some extended time with Him. If you have never had a consistent time with God I would encourage you to read one chapter of Scripture each day. Then spend at least five minutes praying about what God has taught you in that chapter, the needs of your family, and other items on your schedule. There are many books on prayer to help you grow in your communication with God.

149 Parsons Bible Illustrator (Hiawatha, Iowa: Parsons Technology, 1991).

150 World Book Encyclopedia, 1993 edition, Volume 20, p. 261.

151 From 1 Samuel 15:22. The context of 1 Samuel 15:22 is much different than what I am referring to at this point. I am discussing the topic of loving God whereas in that setting the context was one of disobedience verses obedience. Yet the phrase is appropriate for the current setting.

152 Other verses include Deuteronomy 5:10; 7:9; 11:1; 30:16; Joshua 22:5; Jeremiah 1:5; Daniel 9:4.

153 Romans 12:2.

154 There are many Scriptures about loving others, especially brothers and sisters in Christ. The most famous of these passages is probably 1 Corinthians 13. Matthew 5:44 tells us that we are to love our enemies and pray for those who persecute us. Many other

sections reflect that we should love one another because of God's love for us through His Son, Jesus Christ. The following are a few New Testament verses reminding us to love others. John 13:34; Romans 12:10; 13:8-9; Galatians 5:13; Ephesians 4:2; 1 Thessalonians 3:12; 4:9; 5:13; 2 Thessalonians 1:3; Hebrews 10:24; 1 Peter 1:22; 4:8; 1 John 3:11, 23; 4:7-12, 19-21; 2 John 1:5.

155 William Shakespeare, King Henry the Eighth, The Complete Works, ed. (England: Omega Books, 1987).

156 Colossians 3:12-13.

157 As I understand Scripture, according to the verses I have sighted above, a person is not truly a believer in Jesus Christ if he or she refuses to forgive someone else. People may struggle to forgive others who have hurt them and still be believers. But to be unrepentant and admittedly continue in bitterness is evidence people have not had a change of heart.

I realize this is a controversial statement, and many apply the unwillingness to forgive with carnality (not walking with Christ) rather than to salvation. Yet because of the forceful statements made by Paul and Jesus, I can't take the safer path of "fellowship with God" versus "the forgiveness of God." If people have truly had a change of heart and been made new creatures in Christ, then they will understand God's forgiveness towards them is so incredible that they will willingly, by faith, forgive others unconditionally (even in extreme cases such as abuse, rape, slander, fraud, etc.).

Like the fornicator, homosexual, and covetous person who continues in sin with an unrepentant heart, the person who is unwilling to forgive will not inherit the kingdom of God (1 Corinthians 6:9 and Galatians 5:19-21).

We may not always *feel* forgiveness, and usually we are not under any mandate to continue befriending people who hurt us. As the saying goes, "Fool me once, shame on you. Fool me twice, shame on me." Yet we must ask God to help us to forgive them, and then by faith, do it. This is an act of submissive obedience to God. God will use this to set us free from bitterness and hatred as He works healing in our hearts over a short or long period of time.

158 Taken from Parsons Technology Bible Illustrator (Hiawatha, Iowa: Parsons Technology, 1990).

159 Library of World Poetry, William Cullen Bryant, ed., (New York: Chatham River Press, 1984), p.111.

160 Peters and Waterman, In Search of Excellence (New York: Warner Books,) 1982, p. 65.

161 Ibid., p. 279.

162 Ibid., p. 280.

163 Some excellent resources on this topic:

George Barna, Evangelism That Works (Ventura, California: Regal Books, 1995).

Ron Bennett, Intentional Disciplemaking (Colorado Springs, Colorado: NavPress, 2001).

A.B. Bruce, The Training of the Twelve (Edinburgh, Scotland: T & T Clark, 1877).

Robert Coleman, The Master Plan of Evangelism (Old Tappan, New Jersey: Revell, 1980).

Leroy Eims, The Lost Art of Disciple Making (Grand Rapids, Michigan: Zondervan, 1978).

Bill Hull, The Disciple Making Pastor (Old Tappan, New Jersey: Revell, 1988).

Mark Mittelberg, Building a Contagious Church (Grand Rapids, Michigan: Zondervan Publishing House, 2000).

Elmer Towns, ed., The Complete Book of Church Growth (Wheaton, Illinois: Tyndale, 1986). Note especially Chapter 35, "The Priority of the Church."

164 Other versions of the Great Commission are found in Mark 16:15; Luke 24:47; and Acts 1:8. There are many other Scriptures that incorporate the ideas of the Great Commission in both the Old and New Testaments.

165 Bill Hull, Jesus Christ, Disciplemaker (Minneapolis: Church Ministries Department, Free Church Publications, 1988), p. 174.

166 Luke 19:10.

167 Each of these parables is found in Luke 15.

168 I understand that those who have the gift of evangelism consistently share their faith in Jesus Christ to the point of decision with others and see people come to faith in Jesus Christ. Quite often, as with other gifts in the body of Christ, it is hard for these people to understand why others struggle so much with sharing their faith. As with other spiritual gifts, there are many in the body of Christ who have this gift but have never actively developed it. I don't consider myself as having the gift of evangelism. In spite of much training in this area, evangelism has never been easy for me, and I have seldom experienced leading others to Christ. Yet I do desire to be obedient to my Lord in this area of my life, and have people in my life who hold me accountable in this spiritual discipline.

169 Christ is the only way: John 1:12; John 14:6; Acts 4:12; Ephesians 2:1-9; and 1 John 5:11-13. There is eternal punishment: Matthew 25:31-34, 41, 46; 2 Thessalonians 1:8-9; Hebrews 10:29-31; and Revelation 14:10-11; 20:10, 14-15.

170 Leonard Ravenhill, Why Revival Tarries (Minneapolis: Bethany House Publishers, 1959), p. 32.

171 After I heard of Ken's death, I wrote a letter to his wife and told her of Ken praying to receive Christ.

When I later met her personally she told me that when he got home that day from our appointment, he asked his wife (who is a Christian) if she knew whether or not she was going to heaven. He then told her that he was sure he was going to heaven. God had prepared Ken's heart for a divine appointment with Randy and me.

172 Lee Strobel, Inside the Mind of Unchurched Harry & Mary (Grand Rapids, Michigan: Zondervan, 1993), p. 91.

173 Charles R. Swindoll, Strengthening Your Grip (Waco, Texas: Word Books, 1982), p. 235.

174 Romans 1:16-17.

175 I have recently started a ministry called the Johnny Appleseed Club. As Johnny Appleseed sowed many apple seeds because he wanted to bear fruit, so we are to sow seeds of the gospel to bear fruit. This is based upon Mark 4:1-23. This club encourages believers to commit to share the gospel with others. It is basically an accountability group through e-mail. You can find out more about the club by visiting www.lifechangeministries.org.

176 Titus 3:5; 1 Peter 2:1-2.

177 A few verses that remind us of Paul's desire for us and his spiritual children to grow in Christ are: Romans 12:1-2; 1 Corinthians 15:58; Ephesians 6:21-22; Philippians 2:19-30; Colossians 4:12-13; 1 Thessalonians 2:7-12; and 2 Timothy 2:2.

178 There are many good resources to help you lead people in growing in Jesus Christ. A few of these are:

Christopher B. Adsit, Personal Disciplemaking (San Bernadino, California: Here's Life Publishers, 1988).

Leroy Eims, The Lost Art of Disciple Making (Grand Rapids, Michigan: Zondervan, 1978).

Gary Kuhne, The Dynamics of Personal Follow-Up (Grand Rapids, Michigan: Zondervan, 1976).

Growing in Christ (Colorado Springs: NavPress, 1980).

Growing Strong in the Family of God (Colorado Springs: NavPress, 1992).

Your Life in Christ (Colorado Springs: NavPress, 1991).

179 The Greek word for "disciple" is *mathetes* which means "learner or follower." The disciple is someone who sits at the feet of another and learns from that person's life and example. We often hear the term "mentor" when talking of discipleship today. This conveys a less formal relationship in the discipleship process.

180 The word used here for "striving" has as its root *agon* which was the place, like a stadium, where a contest would have been held in the Greek culture. It could also mean the fight or contest that may have been held there. At the stadium the competitors agonized and struggled. Paul fought as if in a battle, to see that these disciples would become mature in Christ. Reference: The New International Dictionary of New Testament Theology, Vol. 1, Colin Brown, ed., (Grand Rapids, MI: Zondervan Publishing House, 1975), pp. 644-648.

181 Here is a sampling of Old Testament passages that speak of God's concern for the world: Genesis 1-3; 6-8; 12:1-5; 45:5; Exodus 3:12-15; Numbers 9:14; 1 Samuel 17:46-47; Nehemiah; Psalm 22:27-28; 47:1-3,7-8; 66; 67; 96; 100; 117; 148:11-14; Isaiah 11:1-12; 25:6-8; 43:8-12; 52:10,15; 55:4-5; 66:18-20; Jeremiah 33:9; Daniel 6:25-28; Jonah; Zechariah 2:11; and many more.

182 Matthew 28:19; Luke 19:10; Acts 1:8; 10:34-48; 13:1, 44-48; Ephesians 2:11-13; Revelation 5:9-10.

183 Acts 11:19.

184 Five students caught in a rain storm at Williams College, Massachusetts in 1806, decided to continue their prayer meeting in a nearby haystack. It was from this episode of prayer concerning foreign missions that the student missionary movement was born. (David Howard, "Student Power," Perspectives on the World Christian Movement A Reader, Ralph Winter and Steven Hawthorne,eds., (Pasadena, California: William Carey Library, 1981), pp. 214-15.

185 D.L. Moody (1837-1899). See footnotes in Chapter 5, "The Obedience of Humility."

186 William Cameron Townsend (1896-1982) founded Wycliffe Bible Translators. As he distributed Spanish Bibles to Indian tribes in Guatemala, he was convicted they should have the Scriptures in their own language. From this humble beginning, thousands of peoples have received the Scriptures in their own language. Reference: Ruth Tucker, From Jerusalem to Irian Jaya (Grand Rapids, Michigan: Zondervan, 1983), pp. 351-357.

187 Information found at www.david.snu.edu.

188 Norm Lewis, Priority One (Orange, California: Promise Publishing Co., 1988), p. 18.

189 Jeremiah 17:13; Isaiah 55:1; John 4:7-15; 7:38.

190 Patrick Johnstone, Operation World (Pasedena, California: William Carey Library, 1993).

191 Cal Thomas, "Dear God, Please Don't Let Me Be a Christian Leader, "Fundamentalist Journal, vol. 3, Issue 5 (May 1984), pages 22-23.

192 Charles Swindoll, Improving Your Serve (Waco, Texas: Word, 1981), p. 34.

193 Charles Swindoll, Living Above the Level of Mediocrity (Waco, Texas: Word, 1987), p. 41.

194 Information taken from International Standard Bible

Encyclopedia, Vol. II, (Grand Rapids, Michigan: Eerdmans, 1988), p. 333.

195 Luke 22:14-30.

196 "Most probably this dispute among the disciples was the immediate cause of the Lord's action in washing their feet, as described in John xiii. When He noticed—we may thus picture the course of events to ourselves—how full of self- seeking and personal ambition His disciples still were, even after all His previous teachings, He stood up without a word, girded Himself and washed their feet (John xiii). When He had finished this and all were again seated quietly round the table, He uttered the words recorded in Luke xxii. 25-30. How forcibly these words would have spoken to the disciples under those circumstances!" Norval Geldenhuys, "The Gospel of Luke," The New International Commentary on the New Testament (Grand Rapids, Michigan: Eerdmans, reprinted, 1983), p. 562.

197 Matthew 23:11; Luke 22:26.

198 James 1:27.

199 Matthew 25:23.

200 Colossians 3:23-24.

201 1 Corinthians 10:31.

202 Acts 20:35.

203 From Parson's Bible Illustrator.

204 If the compliment comes from someone who knows me well, I may ask him to tell me more of what he liked. This can help me improve my speaking, singing, or other gifts. I also ask if there was any thing I could improve. I often ask these questions of my wife when she hears me give a talk or sing. She does a good job giving me helpful evaluations, and I greatly respect her opinion.

205 Jack Mayhall, Discipleship: The Price and the Prize (Wheaton, Illinois: Victor Books, 1984), p. 121.

206 Ephesians 6:11-12, 16; 1 Peter 5:8.

207 "Sound judgment" comes from the Greek *so phroneõ* meaning to be of sound mind or to be temperate. This phrase is also used in 2 Corinthians 5:13, "For if we are beside ourselves, it is for God; if we are of sound mind, it is for you."

208 Psalm 34:2; Jeremiah 9:23-24; 2 Corinthians 10:13-18; 11:5-33; Galatians 6:14; Philippians 3:3-14.

209 Dr. Paul Brand and Philip Yancey, In His Image (Grand Rapids, Michigan: Zondervan, 1984), p. 22.

210 Allen P. Ross, Creation and Blessing (Grand Rapids, Michigan: Baker Book House, 1988), p. 112.

Other helpful commentaries on this passage include:

H.C. Leupold, Exposition of Genesis, Vol. 1 (Grand Rapids, Michigan: Baker Book House, 1942); Derek Kidner, Genesis (Downer's Grove, Illinois: InterVarsity Press, 1967).

211 Josh McDowell, "Take a Good Look at Yourself," Charisma, Vol. 10, March 1985, pp. 42-45.

212 Genesis 1:31.

213 Some verses concerning God's roles for family members are 1 Corinthians 7:1-7; Ephesians 5:18-6:4; and 1 Peter 3:1-7.

214 To begin understanding what your spiritual gifts are, I encourage you to ask, "What do I enjoy doing? What do I have a burden to do? What have I done in the past? Do I have training in any areas of ministry? In what area of ministry would I like to grow in my faith? What things have I done in the past that have been affirmed by others?"

There are also helpful tools such as spiritual gift tests. I currently use the Spiritual Gifts Inventory and Questionnaire from Team Ministry in my own church training. To find out more information concerning this tool, you may write to The Church Growth Institute, P.O. Box 4404, Lynchburg, Virginia, 24502.

215 Ephesians 4:12b-13. See also 1 Corinthians 12:15-20.

216 U.S. News & World Report, May 6, 1996, pp. 8-12.

217 1 Corinthians 6:20; 1 Peter 1:18-19.

218 Romans 3:23-30.

219 A few verses that describe our deliverance from God's wrath through Christ's atonement are Numbers 16:46; Isaiah 53:4-6; Romans 5:8-9; 1 Thessalonians 5:9; and Hebrews 9:11-14.

220 Adapted from Parsons' Bible Illustrator.

221 I often see "help wanted" signs in store windows. But many unemployed workers choose not to work for minimum wage because they can't provide for their families as they wish. Our standards are so high, that these low income jobs aren't appealing. As well, the welfare system has accustomed many to depend on others to provide for their needs. This is not appropriate when a person has the ability to work. Some may have to substantially lower their previous standards, but people shouldn't go without working very long unless it is absolutely necessary. See 2 Thessalonians 3:6-13.

222 "Rhetorically he asks who has made him an arbiter in such matters. The implied answer is that he has no legal standing as a rabbi to do so, but at a deeper level it is suggested that he has a more important mission to fulfill." I. Howard Marshall, Commentary on Luke, New International Greek Testament Commentary (Grand Rapids, Michigan: Eerdmans, 1978), p. 522.

223 Some other passages dealing with the issue of greed are Proverbs 11:6; Romans 1:29; Ephesians 5:3; Colossians 3:5; 1 Thessalonians 2:5; and 2 Peter 2:3, 14.

224 Charles Colson, Kingdoms In Conflict (USA: Morrow & Zondervan, 1987), p. 214.

225 Richard J. Foster, Freedom of Simplicity (San Fransisco: Harper & Row, 1981), p. 87.
226 Philippians 4:11.
227 Philippians 4:13.
228 Philippians 4:10-23.
229 Abraham was 100 years old when God fulfilled His promise to give him his son, Isaac (Genesis 21:5). Moses was 80 years old when God spoke to him at Mount Sinai and told him to lead the people out of Egypt (Acts 7:23, 30). He led the people for 40 more years.
230 Larry Burkett, "Why Retire?," Moody, Vol. 93, No. 4 (December 1992), pp. 26-31.
231 Isaiah 40:7-8; 1 Corinthians 3:10-15; 2 Peter 3:10-13.
232 1 John 2:15-17.
233 1 Timothy 6:6-11.
234 Please notice in verse 21 of Luke 12, "So is the man who lays up treasure for himself, and is not rich toward God," that it doesn't forbid investments for our benefit. The implication of the verse is that the fool made **no** eternal investments. It is not a sin to save for the twilight years. It is not wrong to save for reasonable future expenses such as a car, education, vacations, etc. Please remember, everyone's needs will be different. Yet our savings and spending must be balanced with the idea that we must also be investing in the things of God.
235 Proverbs 22:7.
236 Luke 12:33.
237 Proverbs 30:8-9 reminds us that we are to seek balanced financial lives. The early church gave to meet the needs of others, not so they would create another needy family. God may ask some to give up many or all of their possessions because of their wrongful attitude toward wealth and possessions.

See the story of the rich young ruler in Matthew 19:16-26.

238 1 Timothy 6:6-16.

239 Please read Larry Burkett's, Answers to Your Families Financial questions, pp. 101-123, to find further insight on the principles of tithing and other types of giving.

240 This whole section of Scripture, 2 Corinthians 9:6-15, supports our other conclusions and gives further instruction about financial giving.

241 The word for "cheerful" is the Greek noun *hilaros*, from which we get "hilarity." *Hilaros* has the basic meaning of "cheerful, glad, or merry." It can also include "kind and gracious," which would be appropriate in 2 Corinthians 9:7. Information from F. Wilbur Gingrich and Fredrick W. Danker, A Greek-English Lexicon of the New Testament and Other Early Christian Literature, 2nd edition, revised and augmented, (Chicago: Chicago Press, 1979), p. 375.

242 Luke 21:1-4.

243 Matthew 6:2-4.

244 Lloyd M. Perry and Norman Shawchuck, Revitalizing the Twentieth Century Church (Chicago: Moody Press, 1982), p. 76.

245 Matthew 6:21; Luke 12:34.

246 Burkett, ibid.

247 I am not suggesting that we should agree with every detail and decision of the leadership and congregation of a church or else leave the church. But if we disagree with its basic philosophy of ministry, we should look for another church family. We should be involved with a church where we can be excited about the direction in which God is taking the leadership and the congregation. No church is perfect, but we should feel our church is striving to please God

through the stewardship of its mission and resources.

248 Galatians 6:6-10.

249 Some groups, like the United Way, are an umbrella for hundreds of organizations, some of which a Christian may not want to support. Check with your local organization to see who they specifically support and if you can precisely target your funds to one or more of their organizations.

250 I have only scratched the surface on biblical financial principles. I encourage you to read works by Larry Burkett, Ron Blue, and other respected Christian financial counselors for more insight into this important topic.

251 Chuck Colson, <u>Loving God</u> (Grand Rapids, Michigan: Zondervan, 1983), pp. 24-25.

252 From James 4:10; 1 Peter 5:6.

253 Jack Mayhall, <u>Discipleship: The Price and the Prize</u> (Wheaton, Illinois: Victor Books, 1984), p. 121.

254 Psalm 37:37; Proverbs 29:25; Matthew 23:12; Luke 1:52; 14:11; 18:14; James 4:10; 1 Peter 5:6. The idea of Jesus, the humble servant, being exalted (Isaiah 52:13, and Philippians 2:9) will be discussed in the next chapter.

255 This quote seems to come from Proverbs 3:34, "Though He scoffs at the scoffers, yet He gives grace to the afflicted."

256 James 4:6-10.

257 It is interesting to note that Peter also mentions the need to resist the devil when he examines humility in 1 Peter 5.

258 See <u>Spiritual Warfare</u> by Timothy Warner (Wheaton, Illinois: Crossway Books, 1991), pp. 120-121 for further discussion.

259 I can't set your boundaries nor will I attempt to do so. Some of us are weak where others are strong. But we

must, in humility, be willing to ask God if there are areas of our lives where, for the sake of purity and righteousness before God, we should be more strict. Some have chosen not to watch television or go to movies because of their desire to be holy. It is not wrong to be spiritual for the right reasons. But let us be careful to not be self-righteous, judging others by our own standards, rather than God's.

260 Deuteronomy 23:9; Psalm 34:14; 37:27; 97:10; Romans 12:17, 21; 1 Thessalonians 5:21-22.

261 R. Kent Hughes, James: Faith that Works (Wheaton, Illinois: Crossway Books, 1991), p. 189.

262 D. A. Carson says concerning Matthew 23:11-12, "... 'will be exalted' are pure futures without imperatival force.... The principle enunciated in these verses reflects not natural law but kingdom law: the eschatological reward will humble the self-exalted and exalt the self-humbled, ..." D. A. Carson, The Expositor's Bible Commentary, Vol. 8, Frank Gaebelein, ed. (Grand Rapids, Michigan: Zondervan, 1984), p. 476.

263 D.A. Carson says, "Within the metaphorical world, "life... to the full" suggests, fat contented, flourishing sheep, not terrorized by brigands; outside the narrative world, it means that the life Jesus' true disciples enjoy is not to be construed as more time to fill (merely 'everlasting' life), but life at its scarcely imagined best, life to be lived." D.A. Carson, The Gospel According to John (Grand Rapids: Eerdmans, 1991), p. 385.

264 Micah 6:8.

265 Potiphar was an Egyptian officer in the house of Pharaoh, captain of Pharaoh's bodyguard (Genesis 39:1).

266 Genesis 50:20.

267 Romans 8:28.

268 Dave Brannon, "A Journey Into the Unknown," Sports Spectrum, Vol. 6, No. 2 (March/April 1992), p. 9.

269 Some other verses that remind us of our need to exalt God are Job 37:23; Psalm 18:46; 34:1-3; 46:10; 99:2, 5, 9; 108:5; Isaiah 33:5; Revelation 4:8-11.

270 These doctrines are specifically found in Ephesians 1:3-12.

271 Psalm 75:6-7; 89:16, 17, 19, 24; Proverbs 29:25; Luke 1:52; 1 Peter 5:6; James 4:10.

272 One example is from Numbers 13 and 14. Ten of the twelve spies were unwilling to encourage the people to take what God had given to them because of the Nephilim. Therefore, God did not allow them to occupy the land. Another example is in Joshua 7 and 8. Because of Achan's sin, God did not give the land of Ai to Israel. In both these situations, and others, once Israel walked in obedience and repentance, God allowed them to inhabit the land.

273 See also Psalm 55:22. 1 Peter 5 begins by specifically discussing the humility needed by the leadership of the local church in not "lording over" the people. Peter broadened his application to include the importance of humility in the whole body of Christ. Peter included themes similar to James 4:6-10. The 1 Peter passage is another one where I see reason to believe God means that He will exalt those who are humble in this life, as well as in the life to come.

274 Walter Searle, David Brainerd's Personal Testimony (Grand Rapids, Michigan: Baker Book House, 1978), pp. 90-1.

275 Brother Lawrence, The Practice of the Presence of God (Old Tappan, New Jersey: Fleming H. Revell Company, 1958), p. 38.

276 Marilyn Engle, "MOMS IN TOUCH," The Family Watch, No. 3 (January 17, 1993), Gladstone,

Missouri.

277 Murray, ibid. p. 92.

278 Information taken from my own watching of that magic moment in baseball history and from the book Out of the Blue by Orel Hershiser and Jerry Jenkins (Brentwood, Tennessee: Woglemuth & Hyatt, 1989).

279 See also Isaiah 52:13 and 53:12. It is only in Philippians 2 and Isaiah 52:13 that "highly exalted" is used in Scripture. Yes, we are exalted as the children of God, but Jesus is "highly exalted" as the Supreme Lord. We also see in Isaiah 52:13-15 the threefold exaltation of Christ through the humility of the cross (v.14), in His resurrection (v. 13b), ascension to the right hand of the Father (v. 13c), and the coming of His Kingdom (v. 15).

280 Psalm 16:10; 49:15; Isaiah 53:10-12.

281 Matthew 12:38-40; Mark 9:9-10; John 2:19-22.

282 Other verses pointing to the importance of the resurrection in proclaiming Jesus as the Son of God are Acts 13:29-39; 17:30-31; Romans 1:3-4; 10:9-10; and 14:9.

283 Romans 8:34; Ephesians 1:20-22; Hebrews 1:3; 7:25; 8:1-6; 9:24.

284 Wayne Grudem, "States of Jesus Christ," Evangelical Dictionary of Theology, Walter A. Elwell, ed. (Grand Rapids, Michigan: Baker Book House, 1985), p. 1054.

285 Isaiah 45:22-23; Acts 1:11; Revelation 1:7; 19:11-21.

286 1 Thessalonians 4:16-18; Revelation 20:4.

287 I understand this passage, along with many others, to speak of a millennial reign of Christ. At each point in this phraseology, there is a passage of time before the next phrase takes effect. Thus the millennial kingdom takes place between the phrases, "after that those who are Christ's at His coming," and "then comes the end, when He delivers up the kingdom to the God and

Father,...." In this passage, we see two reasons for the millennial reign of Christ: 1) that He might abolish all other rulers, and 2) that He might deliver the kingdom to His Father.

288 Adapted from Lectures to My Students, by Charles Haddon Spurgeon (Grand Rapids, Michigan: Ministry Resources Library, Zondervan, 1954), p. 377.

289 John 14:1-3; 1 Thessalonians 4:17; 5:8-9.

290 Job 20:15; 1 Corinthians 15:35-49; 2 Corinthians 5:1-4; Philippians 3:20-21; 1 Thessalonians 4:16-17; 1 John 3:2.

291 Revelation 21:18, 21.

292 Isaiah 65:19; Revelation 21:4.

293 Romans 7:14-25.

294 Ephesians 6:10-12; 1 Peter 5:8.

295 Genesis 3:15.

296 Traditionally, the train of a robe, as in a wedding gown or royal garb, was a pronouncement concerning the majesty and importance of the figure wearing the robe.

297 Jonathan Edwards, "Thoughts on Revival," The Works of Jonathan Edwards, Vol. 1, (Carlisle, Pennsylvania: The Banner of Truth Trust, 1984), p. 399.

298 A. W. Tozer, The Pursuit of God (Harrisburg, Pennsylvania: Christian Publications, Mass Market Edition), p. 102.

299 1 Peter 5:6-7.

Printed in the United States
1395300001B/184-231

9 781591 607960